AF488165

FAST TRACK POWER BI

A JOURNEY TO BIA (BEGINNER, INTERMEDIATE , ADVANCE)

RAJESH GURRAM

Copyright © Rajesh Gurram
All Rights Reserved.

This book has been self-published with all reasonable efforts taken to make the material error-free by the author. No part of this book shall be used, reproduced in any manner whatsoever without written permission from the author, except in the case of brief quotations embodied in critical articles and reviews.

The Author of this book is solely responsible and liable for its content including but not limited to the views, representations, descriptions, statements, information, opinions and references ["Content"]. The Content of this book shall not constitute or be construed or deemed to reflect the opinion or expression of the Publisher or Editor. Neither the Publisher nor Editor endorse or approve the Content of this book or guarantee the reliability, accuracy or completeness of the Content published herein and do not make any representations or warranties of any kind, express or implied, including but not limited to the implied warranties of merchantability, fitness for a particular purpose. The Publisher and Editor shall not be liable whatsoever for any errors, omissions, whether such errors or omissions result from negligence, accident, or any other cause or claims for loss or damages of any kind, including without limitation, indirect or consequential loss or damage arising out of use, inability to use, or about the reliability, accuracy or sufficiency of the information contained in this book.

Made with ♥ on the Notion Press Platform
www.notionpress.com

Contents

Chapter 5: Power BI Interface and Components

- 5.1 Power BI Desktop Layout
- 5.1.1 Fields Pane, Visualizations Pane, Filters Pane
- 5.2 Report View, Data View, and Model View
- 5.3 Introduction to Power BI Service
- 5.3.1 Creating Dashboards and Sharing Reports
- 5.4 Power BI Mobile Overview

Chapter 6: Visualizations in Power BI

- 6.1 Types of Visualizations
- 6.1.1 Bar, Line, and Pie Charts
- 6.1.2 Scatter Plots and Maps
- 6.1.3 Matrix and Table Visuals
- 6.2 Custom Visuals and Marketplace Options
- 6.3 Formatting and Customizing Visuals
- 6.4 Best Practices for Effective Visual Design

Chapter 7: DAX Fundamentals

- 7.1 Introduction to DAX (Data Analysis Expressions)
- 7.2 DAX Syntax and Operators
- 7.3 Row Context vs. Filter Context
- 7.4 Common DAX Functions with Examples
- 7.4.1 Aggregation: SUM, AVERAGE, MIN, MAX
- 7.4.2 Time Intelligence: DATESYTD, SAMEPERIODLASTYEAR
- 7.4.3 Logical and Conditional: IF, SWITCH
- 7.4.4 Context Modification: CALCULATE, FILTER

Chapter 8: Advanced DAX

- 8.1 Using Variables in DAX
- 8.2 Iterative Functions: SUMX, AVERAGEX
- 8.3 RANK and Ranking Techniques
- 8.4 Creating Complex Measures with Multiple Filters

Chapter 9: Custom Columns and Measures in Power BI

- 9.1 Understanding Calculated Columns vs. Measures
- 9.2 Creating Custom Columns (Examples and Syntax)
- 9.2.1 Text Concatenation
- 9.2.2 Conditional Columns with IF Statements
- 9.3 Writing Measures with DAX
- 9.3.1 Basic Measure Examples
- 9.3.2 Dynamic Measures Based on User Interaction
- 9.3.3 Example Code for Common Business Calculations

Chapter 10: Data Storytelling with Power BI Dashboards

- 10.1 Designing a Dashboard with Purpose
- 10.2 Adding Interactivity with Slicers and Drill-throughs
- 10.3 Bookmarks and Report Navigation
- 10.4 Sharing and Publishing Reports
- 10.4.1 Power BI Service
- 10.4.2 Exporting and Embedding Options

Preface

ABOUT AUTHOR :

I am Rajesh Gurram....

With over a decade of rich experience in Business Intelligence, I am the author of a QlikBook and have worked with top multinational companies, leveraging my expertise to drive data insights and build powerful BI solutions. My journey spans hands-on mastery in BI tools, including Power BI and Qlik, aimed at empowering businesses with data-driven strategies.

This book is your comprehensive guide to becoming a modern PowerBI Developer, transforming you from a beginner to a hero. Upon completing this book, you'll be well-prepared to tackle real-time projects. It provides a clear learning path, guiding you from beginner to intermediate to advanced levels. While the book thoroughly covers BI tool concepts, it's essential to practice with example data to fully grasp the material.

All the best........... Happy Learning........

I

Chapter 1: Introduction to Power BI Architecture

1.1 Overview of Power BI Ecosystem

Power BI is a suite of tools that enables users to connect, transform, visualize, and share data insights. It includes several components, each with its own role in the data analysis lifecycle:

Power BI Desktop: The main authoring tool, used to connect to data sources, transform data, and create interactive reports.

Power BI Service: A cloud-based platform for sharing, publishing, and collaborating on reports and dashboards.

Power BI Mobile: Mobile apps available for iOS, Android, and Windows that allow users to view and interact with reports on the go.

This ecosystem enables seamless end-to-end data analysis, from raw data to insightful visualizations.

1.2 Power BI Architecture Explained

Power BI's architecture is designed to support scalable data analysis, from local data processing to cloud-based sharing and collaboration. Let's break down the primary components and data flow in a Power BI architecture.

1.2.1 Key Components

Data Sources: Includes on-premises databases, cloud databases, Excel files, and web data.

Data Gateway: Connects Power BI to on-premises data sources securely.

Power BI Desktop: Allows users to design data models, create reports, and implement DAX for custom calculations.

Power BI Service: Provides a platform for report and dashboard sharing, allowing cloud-based data storage and report collaboration.

Power BI Mobile: Offers on-the-go access to reports and dashboards for remote users.

1.2.2 Data Flow from Source to Visualization

The data flow in Power BI can be visualized as follows:

Data Connection: Power BI Desktop connects to various data sources, whether on-premises or cloud-based.

Data Transformation: Power Query Editor cleans, shapes, and transforms data before loading it into the model.

Data Modeling: Relationships and calculations are built using the Data Model, optimizing data for reporting.

Visualization: Reports and dashboards are created, offering interactive visuals and insights.

Sharing: Reports are published to the Power BI Service for sharing and collaboration.

1.2.3 Diagram of Power BI Architecture

Diagram of Power BI Architecture

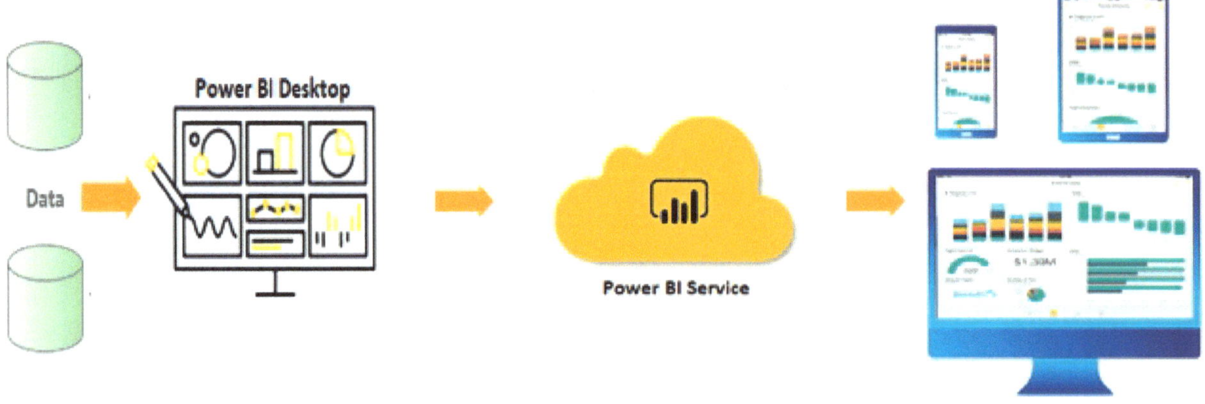

Data Sources → Power BI Desktop → Power BI Service → Power BI Mobile

1.3 Data Importing Techniques

Power BI supports importing data from a wide range of sources, providing flexibility in connecting to different databases, online services, and files.

1.3.1 Connecting to Files

Excel: One of the most common data sources; allows importing entire sheets, tables, and ranges.

Example: Get Data > Excel Workbook > Select Table/Range > Load

CSV and Text Files: Simple flat files; each row is treated as a new record.

XML and JSON: Used for hierarchical data structures and API-based data.

1.3.2 Database Connections

SQL Server: Power BI can directly connect to SQL databases, allowing for complex queries.

Example: Get Data > SQL Server Database > Enter Server and Database Name

Azure SQL Database and Data Lake: Power BI integrates with Microsoft's cloud databases for scalable solutions.

Other Databases: Connections to Oracle, MySQL, etc., are supported, enhancing Power BI's flexibility.

1.3.3 Online Services and API Connections

Microsoft Dynamics 365: Native connectors allow pulling CRM and ERP data.

Google Analytics and Facebook: Access to marketing and social media data.

REST APIs: With Power BI's Web API connector, data can be pulled from various APIs by specifying endpoints and authentication tokens.

Sample Code and Example for Data Importing

Here is an example code for importing data from a web API using Power Query's advanced editor:

```
M                                                                              |

let
    Source = Json.Document(Web.Contents("https://api.example.com/data")),
    Data = Source[Data]
in
    Data
```

(Explanation: This code connects to a web API endpoint, retrieves JSON data, and loads it as a table.)

1.4 Hands-On Exercise: Importing Data and Setting Up a Basic Report
Objective: To import a dataset, transform it, and create a basic report with Power BI.
Import Data: Connect to an Excel file with sample sales data.
Transform Data: Use Power Query to filter out unnecessary columns and rows.
Load Data into Power BI Desktop.
Create a Simple Visualization: Add a bar chart to visualize total sales by product.

Summary of Chapter 1

In this chapter, you learned, with each section introducing critical concepts, sample code, and visuals to enhance understanding the Power BI Architecture and Power BI Services.

II

Chapter 2: Data Transformation Techniques

2.1 Introduction to Power Query

Power Query is a powerful data transformation tool within Power BI that allows you to clean, reshape, and prepare data for analysis. It offers a user-friendly interface for applying various transformations without writing code, although advanced users can use the M language for custom transformations.

2.2 Data Cleansing and Shaping

Cleaning and shaping data is essential to ensure accurate, efficient analysis. Here are common data cleansing steps you can perform in Power Query:

2.2.1 Removing Duplicates

Objective: To remove any repeated rows in a dataset, ensuring unique entries.

Steps:

Select the column(s) with potential duplicate entries.

Click on Remove Duplicates from the Home tab.

Power Query will remove any rows with repeated values in the selected columns.

Original Dataset with Duplicates

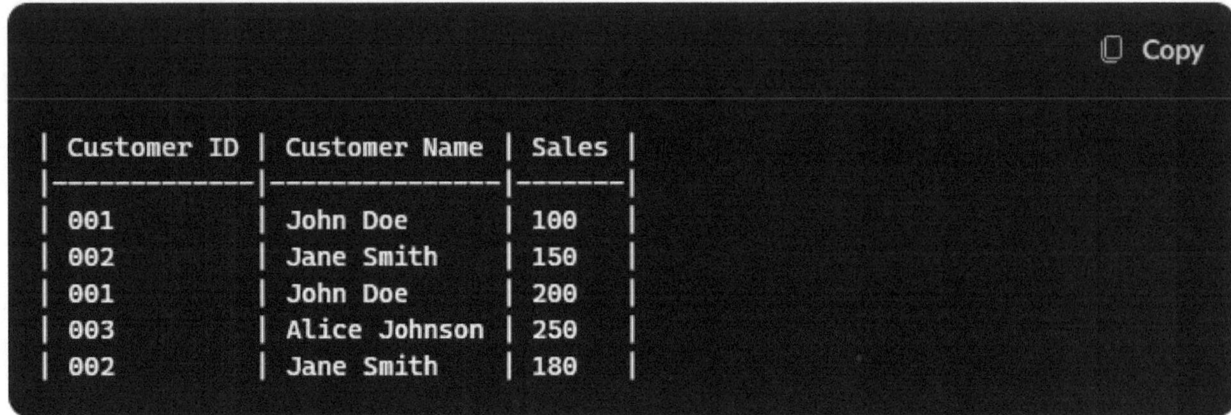

```
| Customer ID | Customer Name | Sales |
|-------------|---------------|-------|
| 001         | John Doe      | 100   |
| 002         | Jane Smith    | 150   |
| 001         | John Doe      | 200   |
| 003         | Alice Johnson | 250   |
| 002         | Jane Smith    | 180   |
```

Dataset After Removing Duplicates

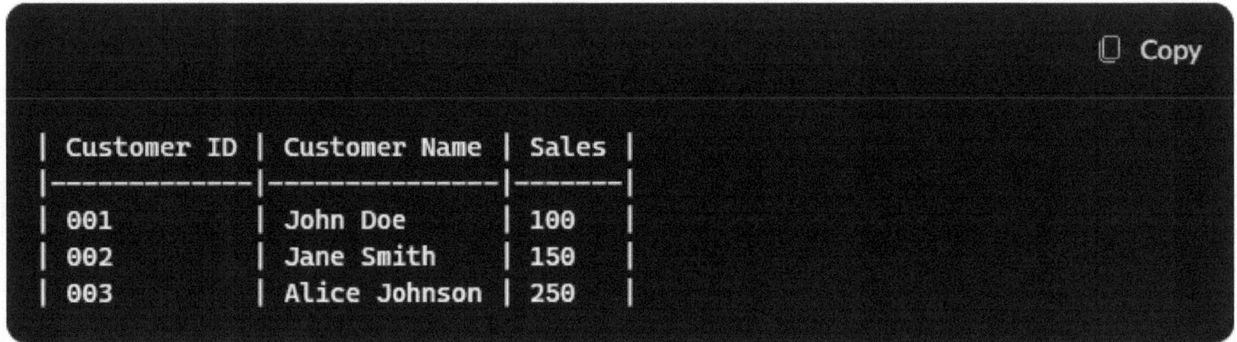

```
| Customer ID | Customer Name | Sales |
|-------------|---------------|-------|
| 001         | John Doe      | 100   |
| 002         | Jane Smith    | 150   |
| 003         | Alice Johnson | 250   |
```

Dataset with duplicate values in a "Customer ID" column and the result after removing duplicates.

2.2.2 Trimming and Cleaning Data

Objective: Remove unnecessary spaces or special characters that may cause issues in analysis.

Steps:

Select the column you wish to clean.

From the Transform tab, choose Trim to remove extra spaces or Clean to remove non-printable characters.

2.2.3 Splitting and Merging Columns

Objective: Divide or combine data in columns for better structure and analysis.

Example: Split a "Full Name" column into "First Name" and "Last Name" columns.

Steps:

Select the column, click Split Column in the Transform tab, then choose By Delimiter.

Choose a delimiter (e.g., space) and Power Query will split the column.

Original Dataset

Splitting the "Full Name" Column

1. **Load Your Data**: Ensure your dataset is loaded into Power BI.

2. **Transform Data**: In the Power Query Editor, select the "Full Name" column.

3. **Split Column by Delimiter**:
   - Go to the "Home" tab.
   - Click on "Split Column" > "By Delimiter".
   - Choose "Space" as the delimiter.

4. **Rename Columns**: Rename the resulting columns to "First Name" and "Last Name".

Resulting Dataset

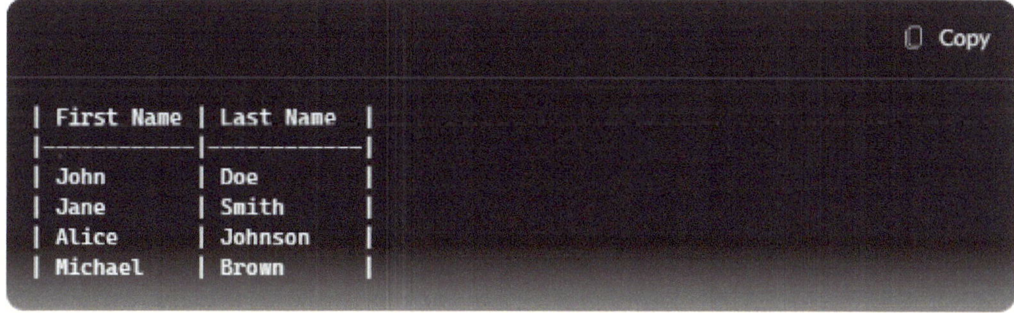

"Full Name" column before and after splitting it into two columns.

2.2.4 Changing Data Types

Objective: Ensuring columns are in the correct data type for accurate calculations.

Steps:

Select the column you wish to update.

In the Home tab, click Data Type and choose the appropriate type (e.g., text, whole number, date).

Original Dataset

```
| Mixed Data      |
|-----------------|
| 2024-01-05      |
| 2024-02-15      |
| Date not set    |
| 2024-03-25      |
| Missing Date    |
```

Steps to Convert Mixed Data Column to Date Data Type

1. **Load Your Data**: Load your dataset into Power BI.

2. **Transform Data**: Open the Power Query Editor.

3. **Replace Non-Date Values**: Replace non-date text values with `null` or a default date. To do this, right-click the column header, select "Replace Values," and replace "Date not set" and "Missing Date" with `null`.

4. **Change Data Type**: Click on the column header, then select "Data Type" and choose "Date."

Resulting Dataset

```
| Mixed Data      |
|-----------------|
| 2024-01-05      |
| 2024-02-15      |
| null            |
| 2024-03-25      |
| null            |
```

column with a mix of date and text formats, then the result after selecting the "Date" data type.

2.3 Advanced Transformations

Power Query offers advanced transformations to handle more complex data preparation needs.

2.3.1 Conditional Columns

Objective: To create columns based on conditions (like "IF" statements).

Example: Classifying sales into "High" or "Low" based on a threshold.

Steps:

Go to Add Column > Conditional Column.

Set conditions, e.g., if "Sales Amount" > 1000, then "High," otherwise "Low."

M

code:

```
// M code for a conditional column = Table.AddColumn(Source, "Sales Category", each if [Sales Amount] > 1000 then "High" else "Low")
```

Original Dataset

Steps to Create "Sales Category" Column

1. **Load Your Data**: Load your dataset into Power BI.

2. **Transform Data**: Open the Power Query Editor.

3. **Add Conditional Column**:

   - Go to the "Add Column" tab.

   - Click on "Conditional Column."

   - Define conditions for the "Sales Category" column. For example:

     - If [Sales Amount] <= 500 then "Low"

     - If [Sales Amount] > 500 and <= 1500 then "Medium"

     - If [Sales Amount] > 1500 then "High"

2.4

Resulting Dataset

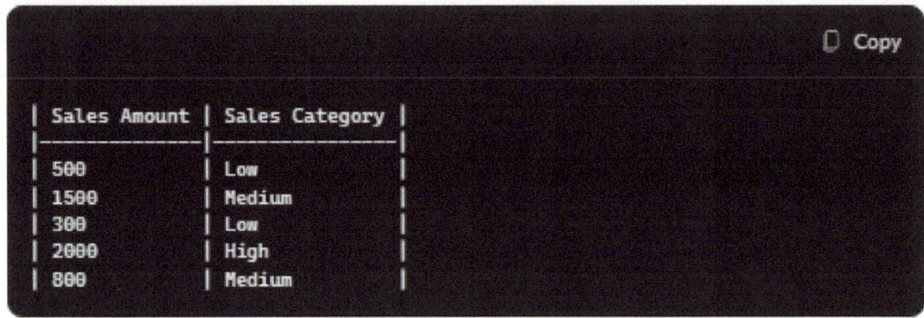

Illustration

Here's an example image depicting this transformation:

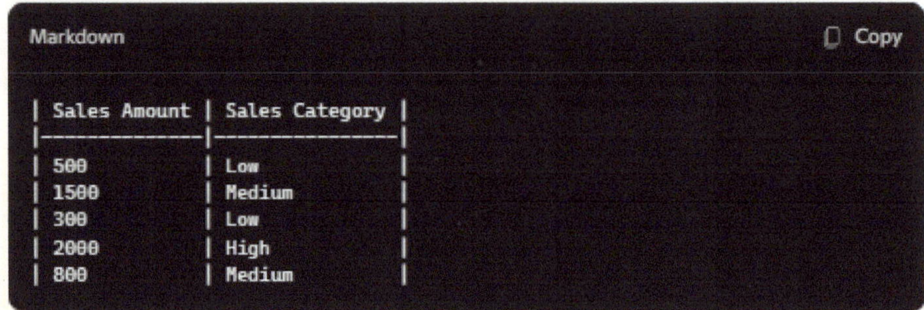

"Sales Amount" column with a newly created "Sales Category" column based on conditions.

2.3.2 Custom Column Formulas

Objective: Create complex calculations using custom formulas.

Example: Adding a 10% increase to all values in a "Price" column.

Steps:

Go to Add Column > Custom Column.

Enter the formula, e.g., [Price] * 1.10.

(Example Code)

M

code:

= Table.AddColumn(Source, "Price Increase", each [Price] * 1.10)

2.3.3 Append and Merge Queries

Append Queries: Combine data from two or more tables into a single table (used when you have similar structure data).

Steps: Go to Home > Append Queries, choose the tables, and combine them.

Merge Queries: Join tables based on key columns, similar to SQL joins.

Steps: Go to Home > Merge Queries, select tables, and specify the matching columns for joining.

Table 1: Product Details

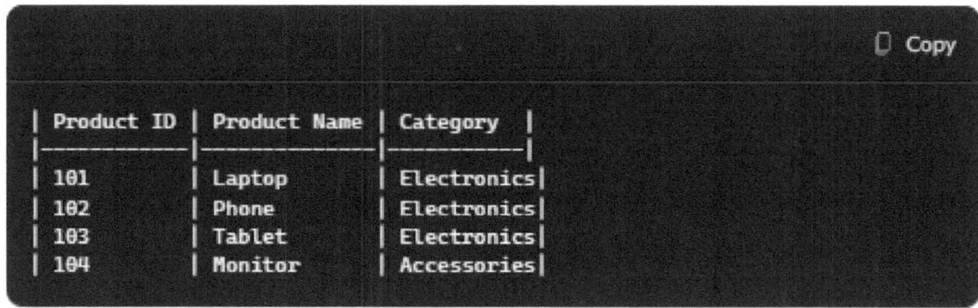

```
| Product ID | Product Name | Category    |
|------------|--------------|-------------|
| 101        | Laptop       | Electronics |
| 102        | Phone        | Electronics |
| 103        | Tablet       | Electronics |
| 104        | Monitor      | Accessories |
```

Table 2: Sales Data

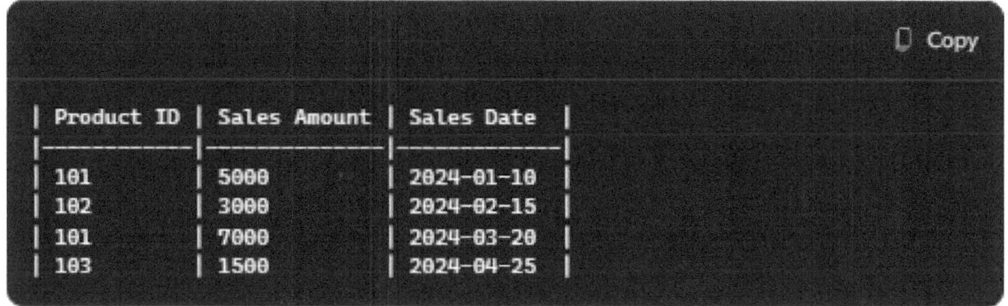

```
| Product ID | Sales Amount | Sales Date |
|------------|--------------|------------|
| 101        | 5000         | 2024-01-10 |
| 102        | 3000         | 2024-02-15 |
| 101        | 7000         | 2024-03-20 |
| 103        | 1500         | 2024-04-25 |
```

Merged Table: Based on "Product ID"

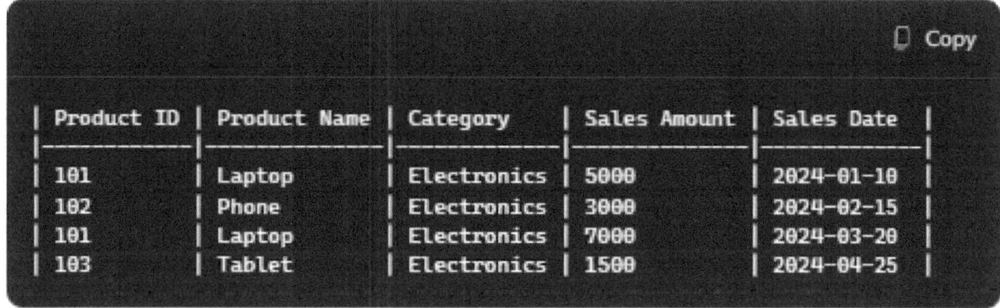

```
| Product ID | Product Name | Category    | Sales Amount | Sales Date |
|------------|--------------|-------------|--------------|------------|
| 101        | Laptop       | Electronics | 5000         | 2024-01-10 |
| 102        | Phone        | Electronics | 3000         | 2024-02-15 |
| 101        | Laptop       | Electronics | 7000         | 2024-03-20 |
| 103        | Tablet       | Electronics | 1500         | 2024-04-25 |
```

Show two tables being merged based on a common "Product ID" column.

2.4 Example of a Data Transformation Process

Let's walk through a scenario where you need to clean a dataset, add calculated columns, and transform it for analysis.

Load the Data: Import an Excel file containing customer sales data.

Clean the Data:

Remove duplicate rows in the "Customer ID" column.

Trim and clean the "Customer Name" column to remove extra spaces.

Transform the Data:

Split the "Date" column into "Year" and "Month" columns.

Create a conditional column called "Order Size" based on the "Quantity" column (e.g., >50 = "Large," otherwise "Small").

Data Type Changes:

Convert the "Sales Amount" column to currency format.

Change "Date" to the date type.

Load into Power BI: Click Close & Apply to load the transformed data into the Power BI Data Model.

2.5 Hands-On Exercise: Data Transformation with Power Query

Objective: Practice data transformation techniques using Power Query to clean and prepare data for analysis.

Steps:

Import Data: Connect to a CSV file containing sales transactions.

Transformations:

Remove duplicates and rename columns.

Add a conditional column to classify transactions by size.

Split the "Product Name" column to separate brand and product type.

Finalize: Apply the transformations and load the data into the model.

Expected Outcome: The cleaned and transformed dataset will be loaded into Power BI for modeling and visualization.

Summary of Chapter 2

In this chapter, you learned how to use Power Query for data transformation. From basic cleansing techniques to advanced transformations like conditional columns and custom formulas, you now have the tools to prepare data effectively in Power BI.

This structure for Chapter 2 includes step-by-step instructions, example code, and images to guide users through Power Query transformations in Power BI. Let me know if you'd like more details on any part or if you'd like to proceed to the next chapter!

III
Chapter 3: Data Modeling Fundamentals

3.1 Introduction to Data Modeling

Data modeling is the process of organizing and structuring data to optimize performance and simplify analysis. A well-structured data model makes it easier to create accurate reports and dashboards by ensuring that data is correctly related and calculations are efficient. Power BI's data modeling tools allow you to create relationships between tables, define calculations, and manage how data flows through the report.

3.2 Cardinality and Table Relationships

Understanding relationships between tables is a fundamental aspect of data modeling. Relationships define how data from multiple tables is combined, which affects the accuracy and performance of analyses.

3.2.1 Types of Relationships

1. One-to-Many (1:M) Relationship:

Commonly used in fact and dimension tables. For instance, a "Sales" table may have multiple rows per "Customer," but each customer appears only once in the "Customers" table.

In Power BI, this is often represented by connecting a primary key in one table (e.g., CustomerID in "Customers") to a foreign key in another (e.g., CustomerID in "Sales").

2. Many-to-One (M:1) Relationship:

Essentially the inverse of the one-to-many relationship and typically represented in a similar way in the data model.

3. Many-to-Many (M: M) Relationship:

More complex and requires careful setup. Used when each value in one table can relate to multiple values in another and vice versa. For instance, in a situation where products can belong to multiple categories and categories can contain multiple products.

Power BI's bidirectional filtering feature enables such relationships but can increase model complexity.

One-to-One (1:1) Relationship:

Rare in BI models, used when each record in one table matches exactly one record in another.

For example, if you have an "Employee" table and an "Employee Contact" table where each employee has one contact record.

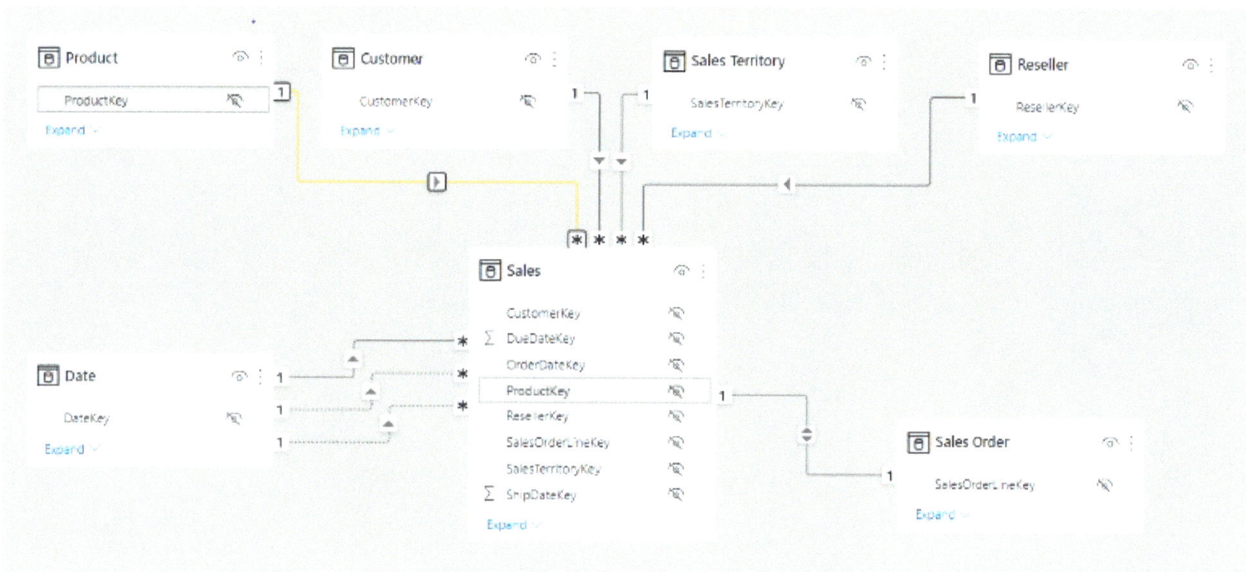

1:M, M:1, M: M, and 1:1 relationships

3.2.2 Real-World Example of Data Modeling

Consider a sample e-commerce dataset with the following tables:

Customers: Contains customer information like CustomerID, Name, and Region.

Products: Lists product details like ProductID, ProductName, and Category.

Sales: A fact table with transaction data, including SaleID, CustomerID, ProductID, Quantity, and SaleAmount.

In this model:

The Customers table has a one-to-many relationship with the Sales table based on CustomerID.

The Products table has a one-to-many relationship with the Sales table based on ProductID.

3.2.3 Best Practices for Building Relationships

Avoid Redundant Relationships: Only create relationships where they're necessary to avoid potential errors in calculations.

Use Primary Keys for One-to-Many Relationships: Ensure that each dimension table has a unique identifier (primary key) for proper connection to the fact table.

Disable Bidirectional Filters When Possible: Although bidirectional filters allow both tables to filter each other, they can complicate the model and slow performance. Use with caution.

3.3 Data Model Optimization

Optimizing a data model involves structuring data efficiently, reducing unnecessary complexity, and using appropriate relationship types for performance.

3.3.1 Avoiding Redundant Columns and Rows

Remove Unnecessary Columns: Exclude columns not needed in reporting to reduce model size and improve performance.

Filter Rows: Use Power Query to limit data to only what is needed for analysis. For instance, if historical data is irrelevant, only load recent years.

3.3.2 Star Schema vs. Snowflake Schema

Star Schema: Consists of a central fact table with direct relationships to dimension tables. This is the recommended schema for Power BI as it improves query performance.

Snowflake Schema: Involves additional layers of dimension tables. While it normalizes data, it can slow down performance and is generally not recommended for Power BI.

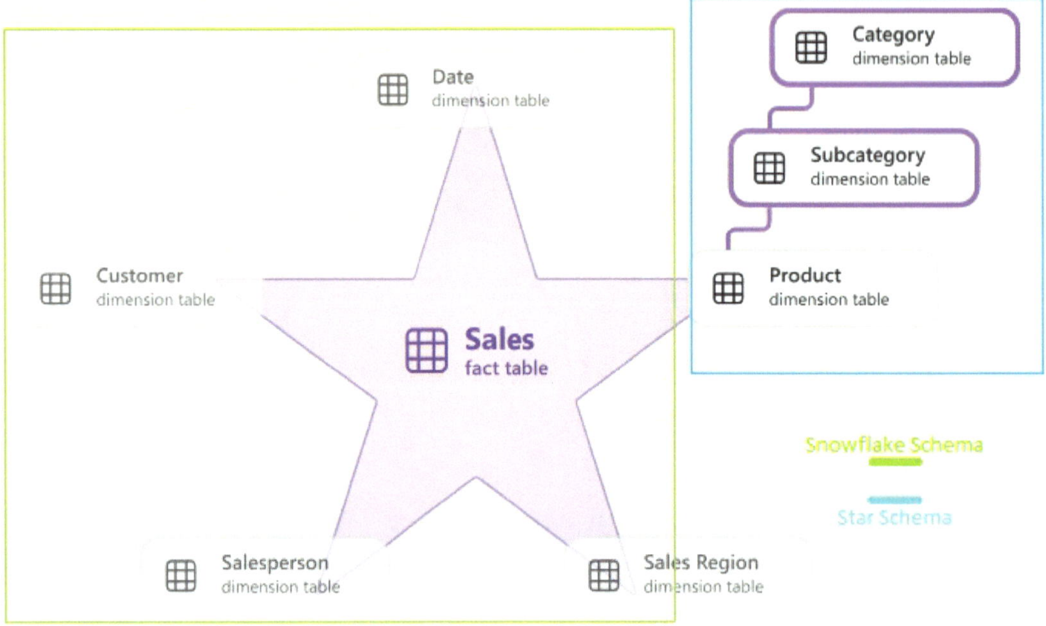

star and snowflake schema

3.3.3 Use of Calculated Columns and Measures

Calculated Columns: Created in the data model to add columns based on row-level calculations. For example, OrderAmount calculated as Quantity * UnitPrice.

Measures: Created in the model using DAX to perform aggregations and calculations that respect the report context. For example, Total Sales = SUM(Sales[SaleAmount]).

3.4 Data Model Best Practices

3.4.1 Naming Conventions and Table Organization

Clear Naming: Use descriptive names for tables, columns, and measures (e.g., "CustomerID" instead of "ID").

Grouping Tables: Group related tables for better organization, such as placing dimension tables like "Products" and "Customers" together.

3.4.2 Measures vs. Calculated Columns

Use Measures for Aggregations: Measures calculate results based on report filters and context, making them efficient for large datasets.

Calculated Columns for Static Data: Only use calculated columns when values won't change across reports (e.g., "Profit Margin" as SaleAmount - CostAmount).

3.4.3 Avoiding Circular Dependencies and Bi-Directional Filters

Circular Dependencies: Avoid configurations where relationships and calculations reference each other in a loop, which can result in errors.

Limit Bi-Directional Filters: Bi-directional filters increase model complexity and should be used sparingly.

3.4.4 Performance Optimization Tips

Minimize Table Sizes: Only load relevant data by filtering in Power Query.

Optimize DAX Formulas: Use efficient DAX functions to reduce calculation time (e.g., using SUMX with appropriate filters).

Aggregate Data When Possible: Aggregate tables at the source or use summary tables when detailed data isn't necessary.

3.5 Example of Creating Relationships and Measures

Here's a step-by-step guide to creating relationships and a sample measure in Power BI:

1. Load the Data: Import tables for Customers, Products, and Sales.

2. Define Relationships:

Open the Model view.

Drag CustomerID from Customers to Sales to create a one-to-many relationship.

Repeat for ProductID from Products to Sales.

3. Create a Measure:

Go to the Sales table, right-click, and select New Measure.

Use DAX to define total sales:

DAX

code:

Total Sales = SUM(Sales[SaleAmount])

Use the Measure in a Visualization: Create a bar chart visual to display Total Sales by ProductName from the Products table.

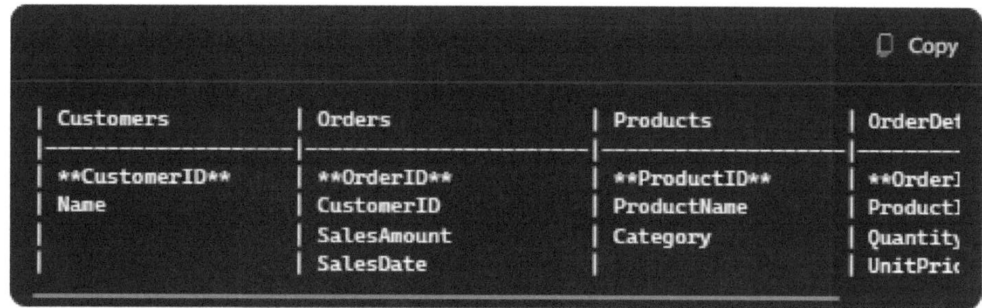

2.6

3.6 Hands-On Exercise: Building Your Data Model

Objective: Set up a data model in Power BI with relationships, calculated columns, and measures.

Steps:

Load the Tables: Import Customers, Products, and Sales tables.

Establish Relationships: Use the model view to connect Customers to Sales and Products to Sales.

Create Calculated Columns:

In the Sales table, add a calculated column called Total Cost as [Quantity] * [UnitCost].

Add Measures:

Create a Total Sales measure and a Total Profit measure (e.g., Total Sales - Total Cost).

Visualize: Create a report page showing total sales and profit by product.

Summary of Chapter 3

In this chapter, you learned the fundamentals of data modeling in Power BI. This included understanding relationships and cardinality, structuring data for efficient analysis, and best practices to optimize model performance. Following these techniques helps build robust data models that enhance the accuracy and performance of Power BI reports.

IV

Chapter 4: Data Visualization Techniques

4.1 Introduction to Power BI Visualization

Data visualization is a key aspect of data analysis that transforms raw data into visual formats, enabling easier interpretation and insights. Power BI offers a range of visualization tools and features to design compelling reports and dashboards. This chapter will guide you through the types of visualizations, how to use them, and best practices for effective data presentation.

4.2 Overview of Power BI Visualizations

Power BI includes a variety of visualizations designed to represent data in different forms. Let's explore the most commonly used visualizations and when to use each one.

4.2.1 Bar and Column Charts

Description: Bar and column charts display data using rectangular bars to represent values.

When to Use: Ideal for comparing categorical data or showing changes over time.

Example: Sales by product category, monthly revenue trends.

4.2.2 Line and Area Charts

Description: Line charts display trends over time, while area charts fill the space beneath the line to show volume.

When to Use: Useful for showing time series data or trends.

Example: Monthly sales trend, stock price changes.

4.2.3 Pie and Donut Charts

Description: Pie and donut charts display data as slices representing parts of a whole.

When to Use: Suitable for showing proportions or percentages.

Example: Market share by region, sales breakdown by product type.

4.2.4 Scatter and Bubble Charts

Description: Scatter plots show relationships between two variables, while bubble charts add a third dimension by size.

When to Use: Ideal for identifying correlations or distribution patterns.

Example: Sales vs. profit by region, customer demographics.

4.2.5 Maps and Geospatial Visualizations

Description: Map visuals plot data on a geographic map, useful for location-based insights.

When to Use: Ideal for geographical data and spatial analysis.

Example: Sales by state, number of stores by city.

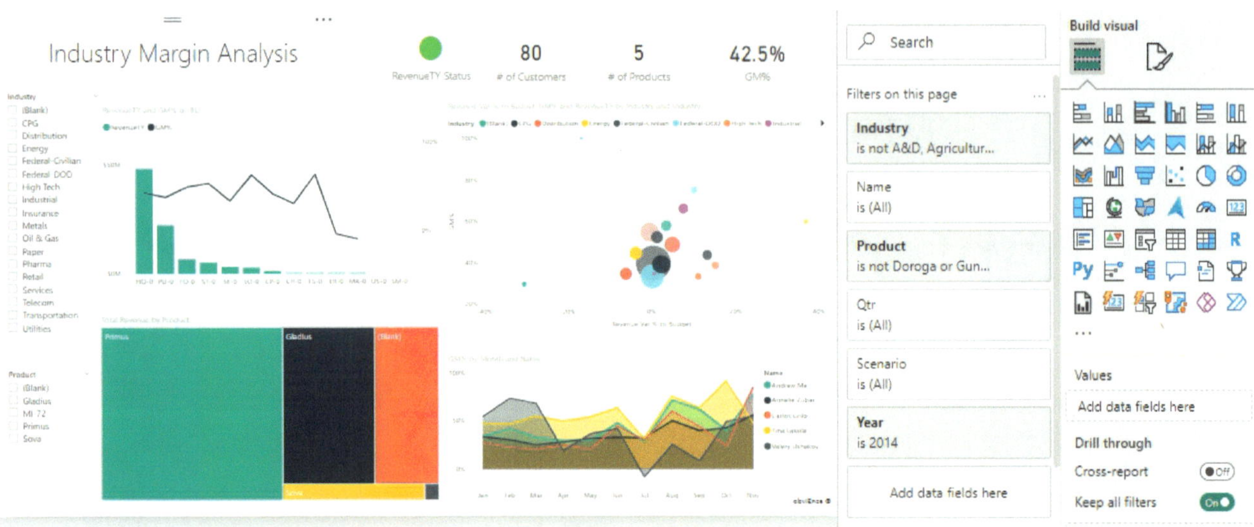

Type of chart

4.3 Creating Visualizations in Power BI

Power BI offers an easy-to-use interface for creating visualizations from data. Here's a general approach to creating and customizing visuals.

4.3.1 Creating a Visualization

Load the Data: Ensure the data is loaded and ready in Power BI Desktop.

Select a Visualization Type: Choose a visual type from the Visualizations pane.

Add Fields: Drag fields from the Fields pane onto the visual to populate it.

For example, for a bar chart, drag a category field (e.g., Product) to the Axis and a value field (e.g., Sales) to the Values.

Customize: Use the Format pane to adjust colors, labels, titles, and more.

process of creating a bar chart

4.3.2 Customizing Visualizations

Data Labels: Turn on data labels to display values directly on the chart.

Titles and Axis Labels: Use descriptive titles and axis labels to enhance clarity.

Color Coding: Apply color coding to distinguish categories, highlight trends, or draw attention to specific data points.

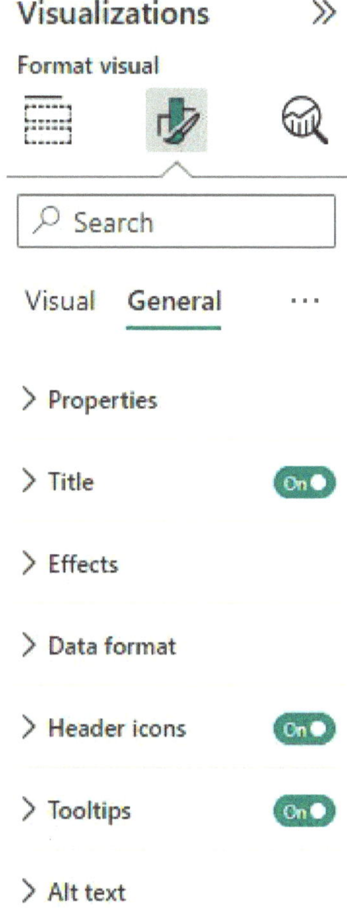

A bar chart with customized labels, titles, and color

4.4 Advanced Visualization Techniques

Power BI also supports advanced visualization techniques to enhance analysis and storytelling.

4.4.1 Drill-Down and Drill-Through

Drill-Down: Allows users to navigate through data hierarchies (e.g., from year to month to day).

Steps: Create a hierarchy by dragging fields into the same axis, then click on Drill Down to explore deeper layers.

Drill-Through: Enables detailed analysis by allowing users to navigate to a report page dedicated to specific details.

Example: Create a drill-through from a summary dashboard to a detailed sales report page for a selected region or product.

4.4.2 Conditional Formatting

Conditional formatting in Power BI enables data-driven styling based on values. Common uses include:

Background Colors: Color cells based on value ranges, such as green for high sales and red for low sales.

Data Bars: Add bars within cells to visually represent values, useful in tables for side-by-side comparison.

4.4.3 Custom Tooltips

Custom tooltips provide additional information when hovering over data points. They are useful for showing contextual data without cluttering visuals.

Example: Show detailed product information when hovering over a bar in a sales chart.

Steps: Go to Format > Tooltip, enable Report Page Tooltip, and customize the tooltip content.

4.5 Best Practices for Data Visualization

Creating effective visualizations is about more than just aesthetics; it's about conveying data insights clearly and accurately. Here are some best practices to follow:

Choose the Right Chart Type: Select visuals that align with the type of data and insights. For example, use line charts for trends and bar charts for categorical comparisons.

Avoid Overloading Visuals: Limit the number of data points and keep charts focused to prevent clutter and maintain clarity.

Use Consistent Colors and Labels: Maintain a consistent color scheme across similar categories and ensure labels are readable.

Highlight Key Data: Use color and size to draw attention to important data points or trends.

Ensure Accessibility: Use high-contrast colors and provide clear labels and tooltips for accessibility.

4.6 DAX for Enhanced Visualizations

Data Analysis Expressions (DAX) are essential for creating custom calculations and measures in Power BI. DAX can enhance visualizations by allowing you to calculate metrics directly within visuals.

4.6.1 Commonly Used DAX Functions for Visualizations

SUM: Adds up values in a column.

Example: Total Sales = SUM(Sales[SaleAmount])

AVERAGE: Calculates the average of a column's values.

Example: Average Sales = AVERAGE(Sales[SaleAmount])

COUNTROWS: Counts the number of rows in a table.

Example: Total Orders = COUNTROWS(Sales)

4.6.2 Dynamic Measures with DAX

Dynamic measures adapt based on user interactions with visuals, such as slicers or filters. For example, create a measure to show year-to-date sales:

DAX

code:

YTD Sales = CALCULATE(SUM(Sales[SaleAmount]), DATESYTD(Sales[Date]))

4.7 Hands-On Exercise: Creating Visualizations with Power BI

Objective: Practice creating and customizing visuals in Power BI for a sales dashboard.

Create Basic Visuals: Add a bar chart for sales by category, a line chart for monthly trends, and a pie chart for sales by region.

Customize Visuals:

Add data labels and axis titles.

Apply conditional formatting to the bar chart.

Add Drill-Through and Tooltips:

Enable drill-through for product details.

Create a tooltip showing additional data for each sales region.

Implement DAX Measures:

Add a Total Sales measure.

Create a Top Product measure to display the best-selling product.

Expected Outcome: A dashboard with interactive visuals that allow users to explore sales data by category, region, and time.

Summary of Chapter 4

In this chapter, we explored the different types of visualizations in Power BI, techniques for customization, and best practices for effective data presentation. Using drill-down, conditional formatting, and DAX, you can create interactive and insightful dashboards tailored to user needs.

V

Chapter 5: Power BI Interface and Components

5.1 Power BI Desktop Layout

Power BI Desktop serves as the primary tool for creating reports, dashboards, and data models. The layout is intuitive, with different sections designed for specific tasks, making it easy to build and manage interactive reports.

5.1.1 Key Interface Elements

Fields Pane:

The Fields pane, located on the right-hand side of the interface, displays all the tables, columns, and calculated fields in your data model.

Drag fields onto the canvas to create visuals.

Right-click options include renaming, hiding, or creating measures and calculated columns.

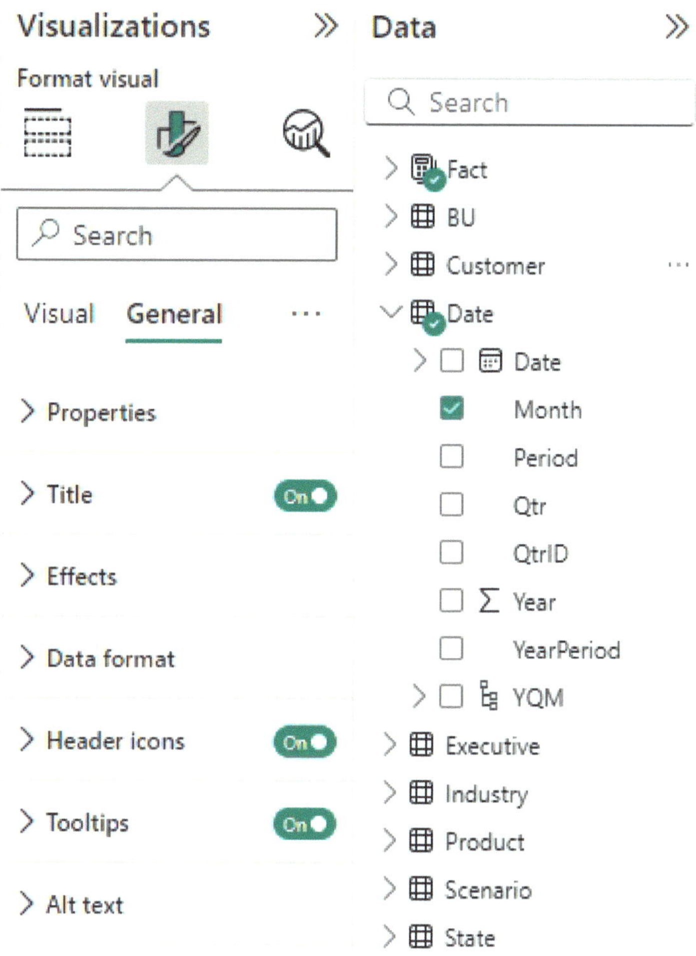

Fields pane with a table and its fields

Visualizations Pane:
This pane offers a wide variety of built-in visuals and customization options.
   Visual Selection: Choose from bar charts, line graphs, pie charts, maps, tables, etc.
   Formatting: Adjust visual properties like colors, labels, legends, and tooltips.
   Interactions: Configure how visuals interact with one another.

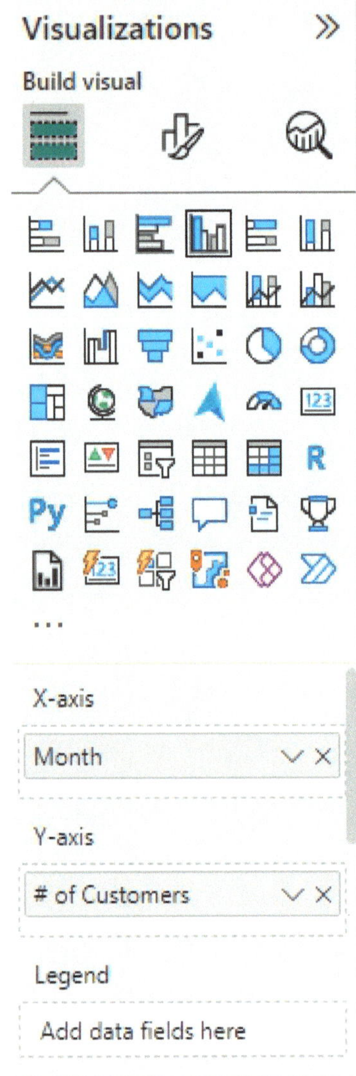

visualizations pane

Filters Pane:

Filters refine data displayed in visuals or across the entire report. Filters can be applied at different levels:

Visual-Level Filters: Apply filters to a specific chart or table.

Page-Level Filters: Impact all visuals on a report page.

Report-Level Filters: Affect all pages in the report.

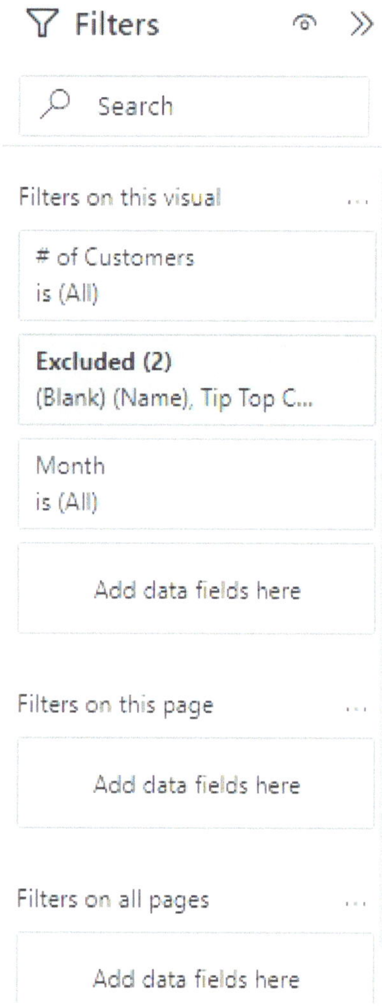

Filters pane

5.2 Report View, Data View, and Model View

Power BI Desktop provides three core views to manage and analyze data. These views are accessible via the icons on the left-hand toolbar.

5.2.1 Report View

The Report View is the default interface for creating and designing reports.

Drag fields and visuals onto the canvas to build interactive reports.

Add multiple pages to your report to organize insights.

Use slicers, filters, and bookmarks to enhance interactivity.

5.2.2 Data View

The Data View allows you to inspect raw data tables imported into Power BI.

Review table contents and identify issues in data quality.

Create calculated columns using DAX to add new insights.

Adjust data types or formatting properties.

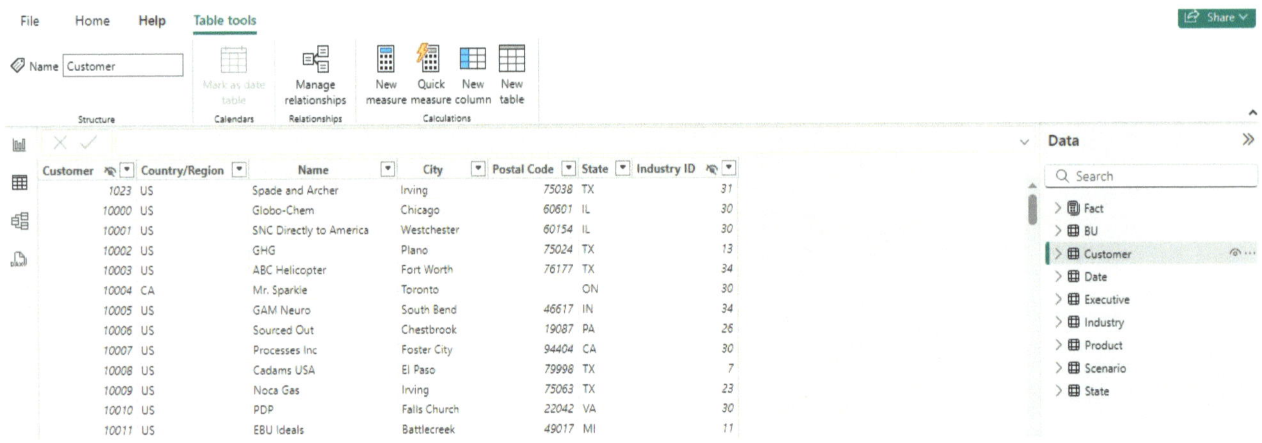

Data View

5.2.3 Model View

The Model View helps you define relationships between tables in your data model.

Visualize table relationships using a diagram layout.

Define relationships using cardinality (e.g., one-to-many or many-to-many).

Configure table properties like primary keys and inactive relationships.

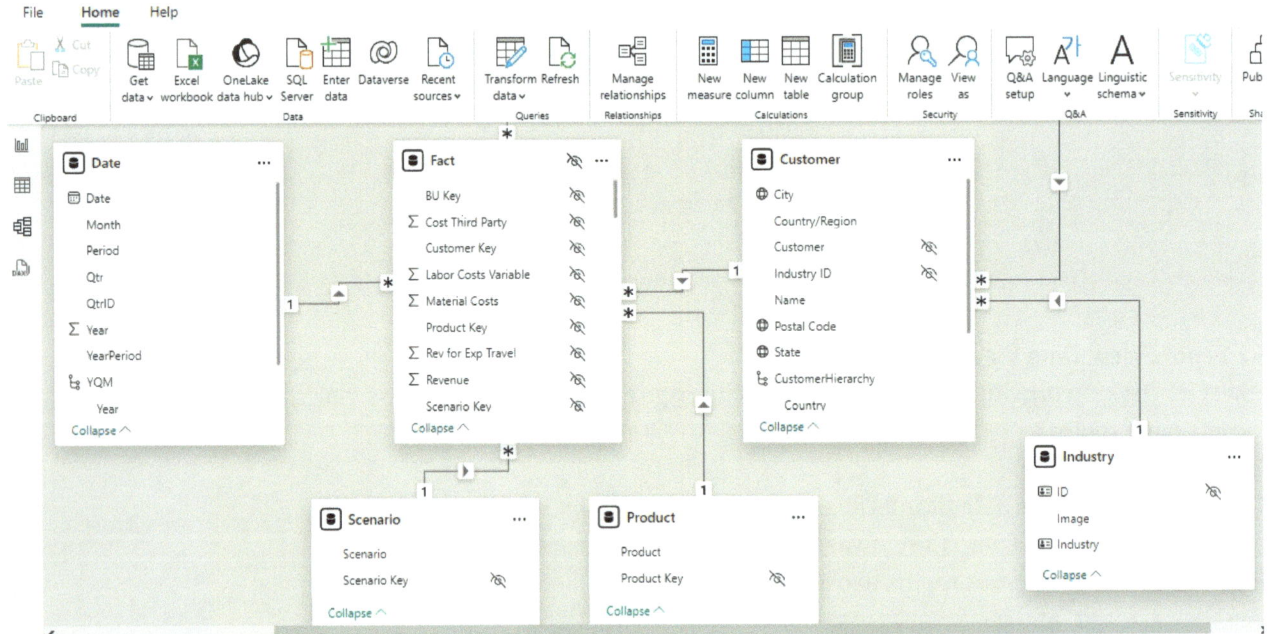

Model View

5.3 Introduction to Power BI Service

Power BI Service is the cloud-based platform for sharing and collaborating on Power BI reports and dashboards. After creating a report in Power BI Desktop, you can publish it to the service for team-wide access.

5.3.1 Creating Dashboards and Sharing Reports

Creating Dashboards:

Dashboards in the Power BI Service are single-page collections of visuals from one or more reports.

Pinning Visuals: Add visuals from reports as live tiles to dashboards.

Custom Tiles: Incorporate text boxes, images, and KPIs to enhance dashboards.

Sharing and Collaboration:

Power BI Service enables collaboration by allowing users to share reports, dashboards, and datasets.

Share reports with individuals or groups within your organization.

Assign roles and permissions to control access.

Use the comment feature to provide feedback or discuss insights with team members.

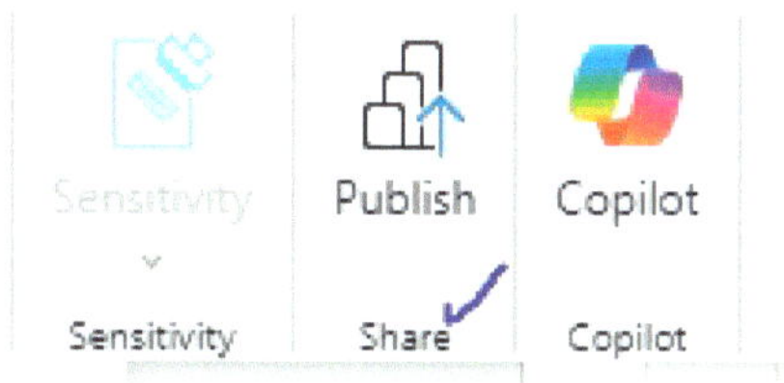

Power BI Service

5.4 Power BI Mobile Overview

The Power BI Mobile app ensures that users can access reports and dashboards on the go. It provides a responsive, touch-friendly interface optimized for smartphones and tablets.

Key Features of Power BI Mobile:

Real-Time Dashboards: Access live data and monitor key metrics in real time.

Interactive Reports: Filter and drill through visuals directly from your mobile device.

Alerts and Notifications: Receive notifications for changes in metrics or thresholds.

Offline Mode: Save reports for offline use during travel or connectivity issues.

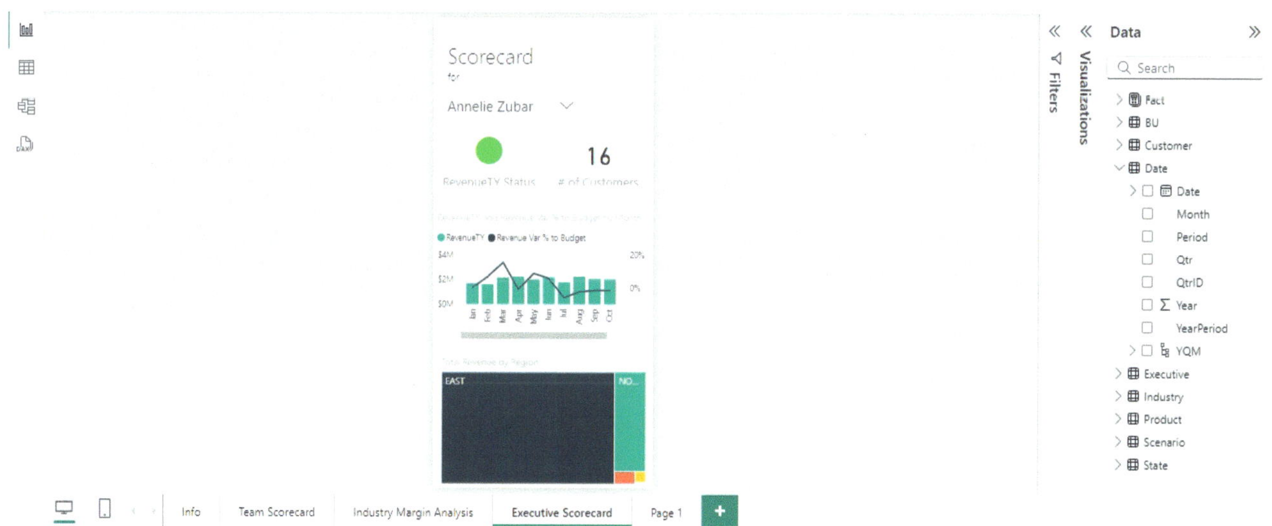

Power BI Mobile app

Use Cases for Power BI Mobile:

Executives tracking business performance metrics on the go.

Field sales teams reviewing regional sales data during client visits.

Teams collaborating in meetings by projecting reports from mobile devices.

Summary of Chapter 5

This chapter provided an overview of the Power BI Desktop layout and its key interface components, including the Fields, Visualizations, and Filters panes. You also explored the three views (Report, Data, and Model View) and their respective functionalities. The Power BI Service was introduced as a platform for collaboration, along with insights into creating dashboards and sharing reports. Finally, the Power BI Mobile app was highlighted as a tool for accessing reports and dashboards on the go.

VI

Chapter 6: Visualizations in Power BI

Visualizations are at the heart of Power BI, transforming raw data into compelling, interactive insights. This chapter explores the types of visualizations available, customization options, and best practices for designing effective visuals.

6.1 Types of Visualizations

Power BI provides a wide range of built-in visuals to accommodate various analytical needs, from basic charts to advanced geospatial maps.

6.1.1 Bar, Line, and Pie Charts

Bar Charts: Represent data using rectangular bars to compare values across categories.

Use Clustered Bar Charts to compare multiple measures across categories.

Use Stacked Bar Charts to show cumulative totals within categories.

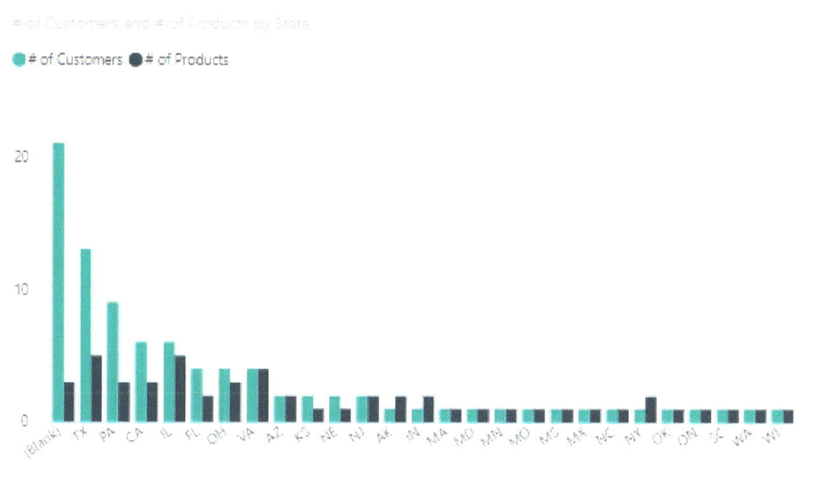

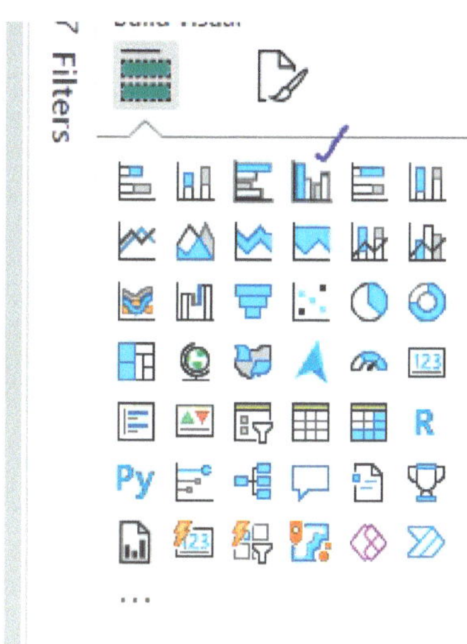

Clustered Bar Chart

Line Charts: Display trends over time or sequential data points using lines.
Ideal for time-series analysis (e.g., monthly sales trends).

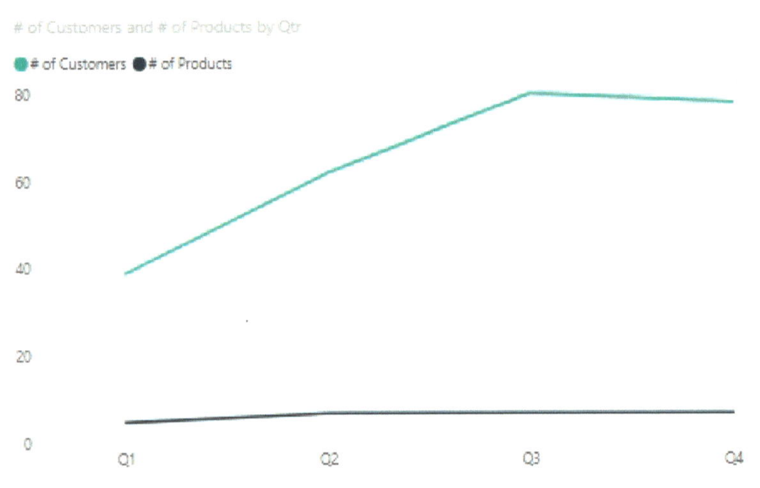
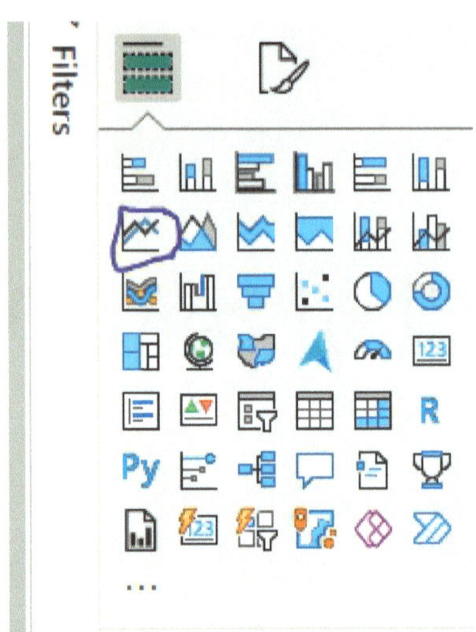

Line Chart

Pie Charts: Show proportions of a whole using slices.
Best for small datasets with limited categories.

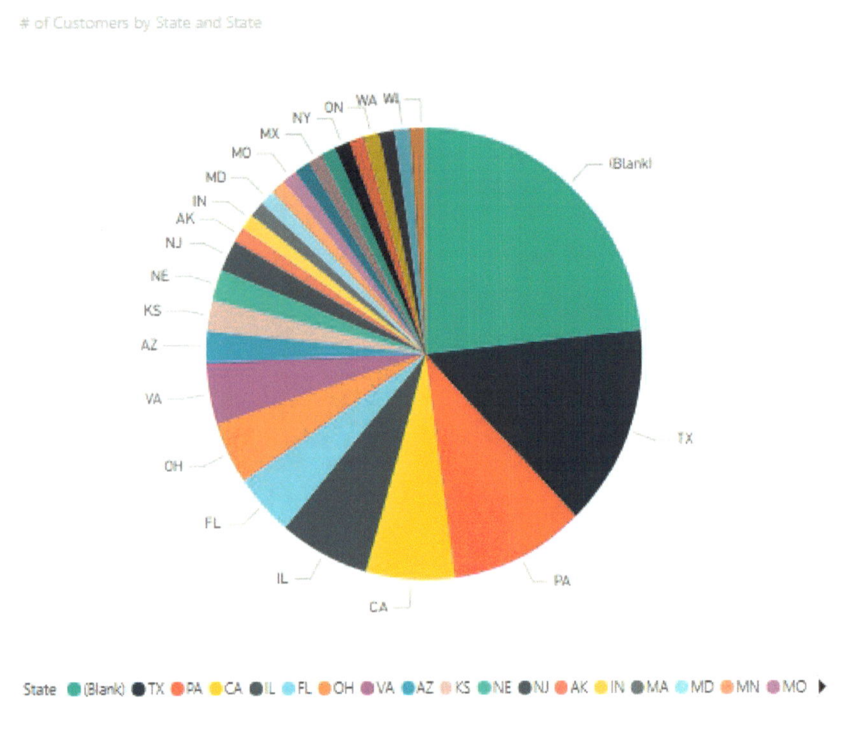
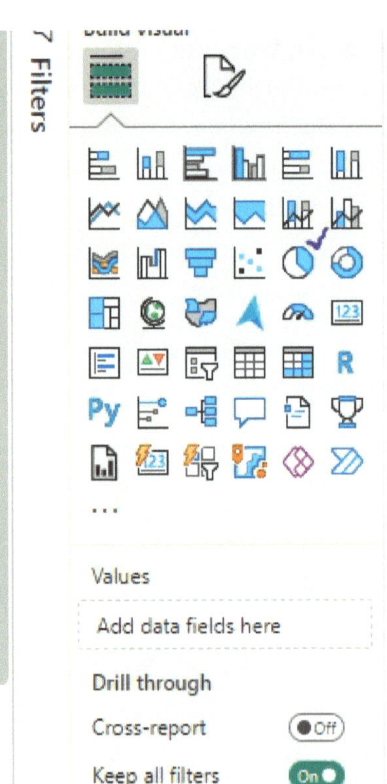

Pie Chart

6.1.2 Scatter Plots and Maps

Scatter Plots: Show relationships or correlations between two numerical variables.
Add a third dimension using bubble size to represent an additional metric.

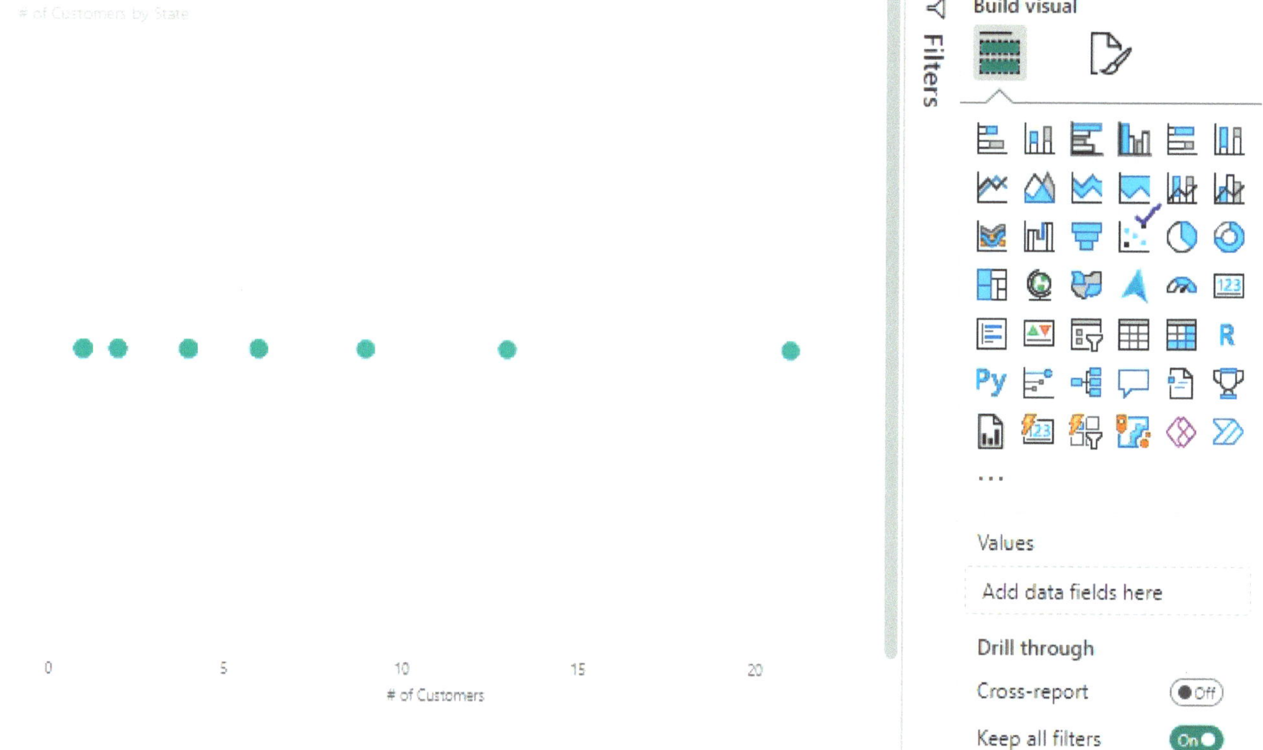

Scatter Plot

Maps: Visualize geographic data with spatial context.
Use Filled Maps for area-based visualizations.
Use Bubble Maps for point-based data.

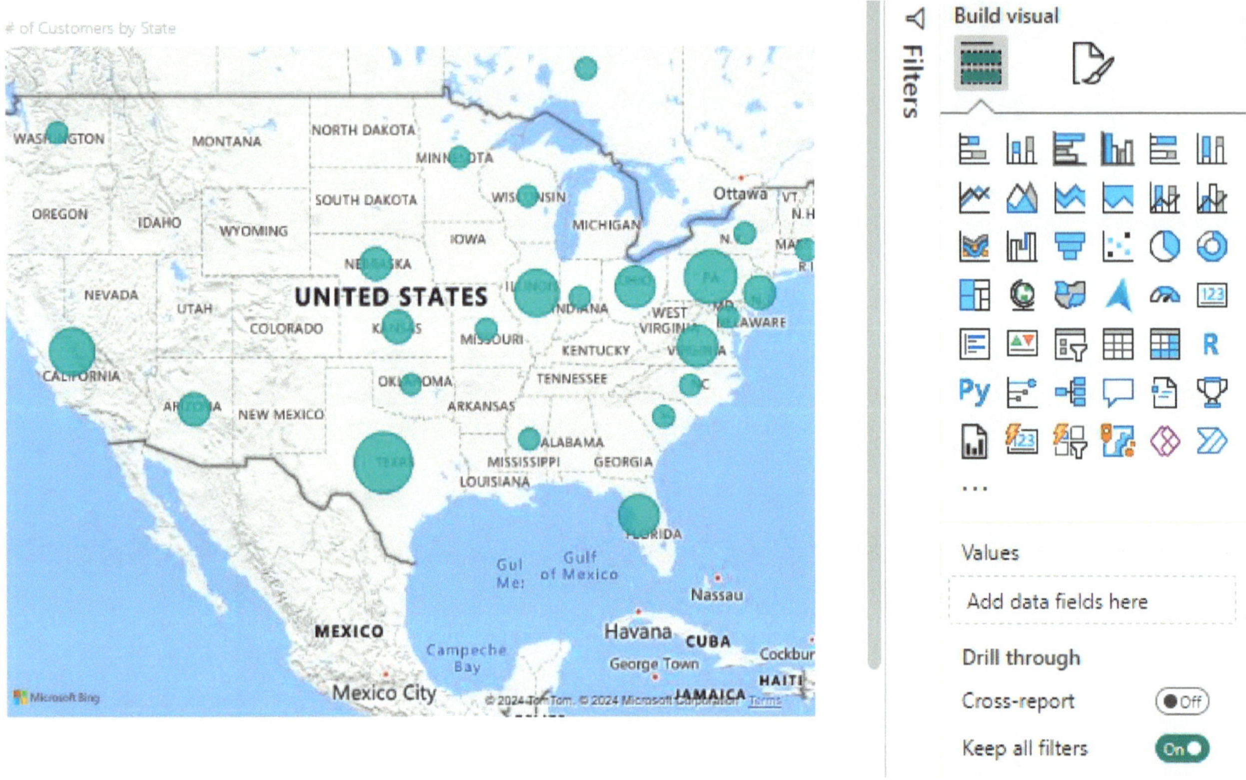

Map

6.1.3 Matrix and Table Visuals

Matrix Visuals: Display data in a pivot-table-like format with rows and columns. Allows for hierarchical grouping and drill-down capabilities.

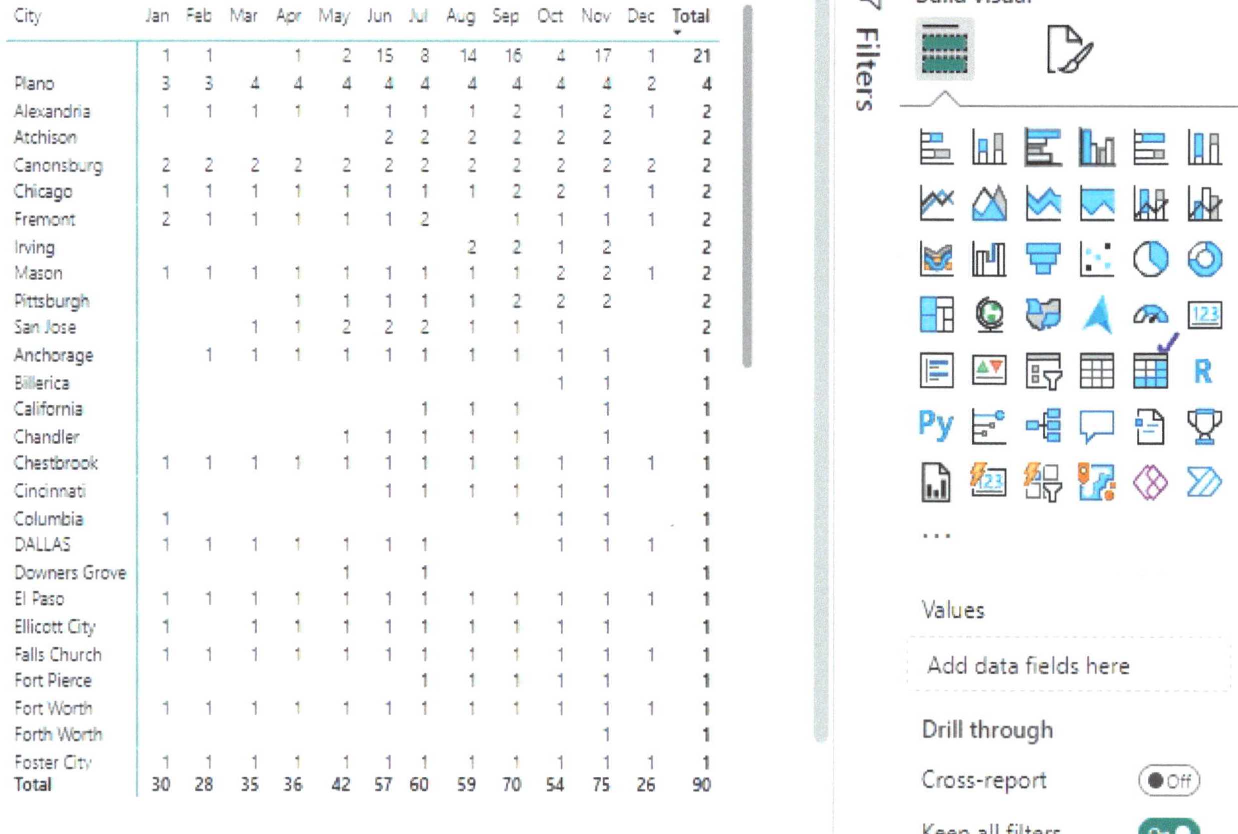

City	Jan	Feb	Mar	Apr	May	Jun	Jul	Aug	Sep	Oct	Nov	Dec	Total
	1	1		1	2	15	8	14	16	4	17	1	21
Plano	3	3	4	4	4	4	4	4	4	4	4	2	4
Alexandria	1	1	1	1	1	1	1	1	2	1	2	1	2
Atchison						2	2	2	2	2	2		2
Canonsburg	2	2	2	2	2	2	2	2	2	2	2	2	2
Chicago	1	1	1	1	1	1	1	1	2	2	1	1	2
Fremont	2	1	1	1	1	1	2		1	1	1	1	2
Irving								2	2	1	2		2
Mason	1	1	1	1	1	1	1	1	1	2	2	1	2
Pittsburgh				1	1	1	1	1	2	2	2		2
San Jose			1	1	2	2	2	1	1	1			2
Anchorage		1	1	1	1	1	1	1	1	1	1		1
Billerica										1	1		1
California						1	1	1			1		1
Chandler					1	1	1	1	1	1			1
Chestbrook	1	1	1	1	1	1	1	1	1	1	1	1	1
Cincinnati						1	1	1		1	1		1
Columbia	1									1	1		1
DALLAS	1	1	1	1	1	1	1			1	1	1	1
Downers Grove						1		1					1
El Paso	1	1	1	1	1	1	1	1	1	1	1	1	1
Ellicott City	1		1	1	1	1	1	1	1	1	1		1
Falls Church	1	1	1	1	1	1	1	1	1	1	1	1	1
Fort Pierce							1	1	1	1	1		1
Fort Worth	1	1	1	1	1	1	1	1	1	1	1	1	1
Forth Worth											1		1
Foster City	1	1	1	1	1	1	1	1	1	1	1	1	1
Total	30	28	35	36	42	57	60	59	70	54	75	26	90

Matrix

Table Visuals: Present raw data in a tabular format with customizable columns. Best for detailed analysis and exporting data.

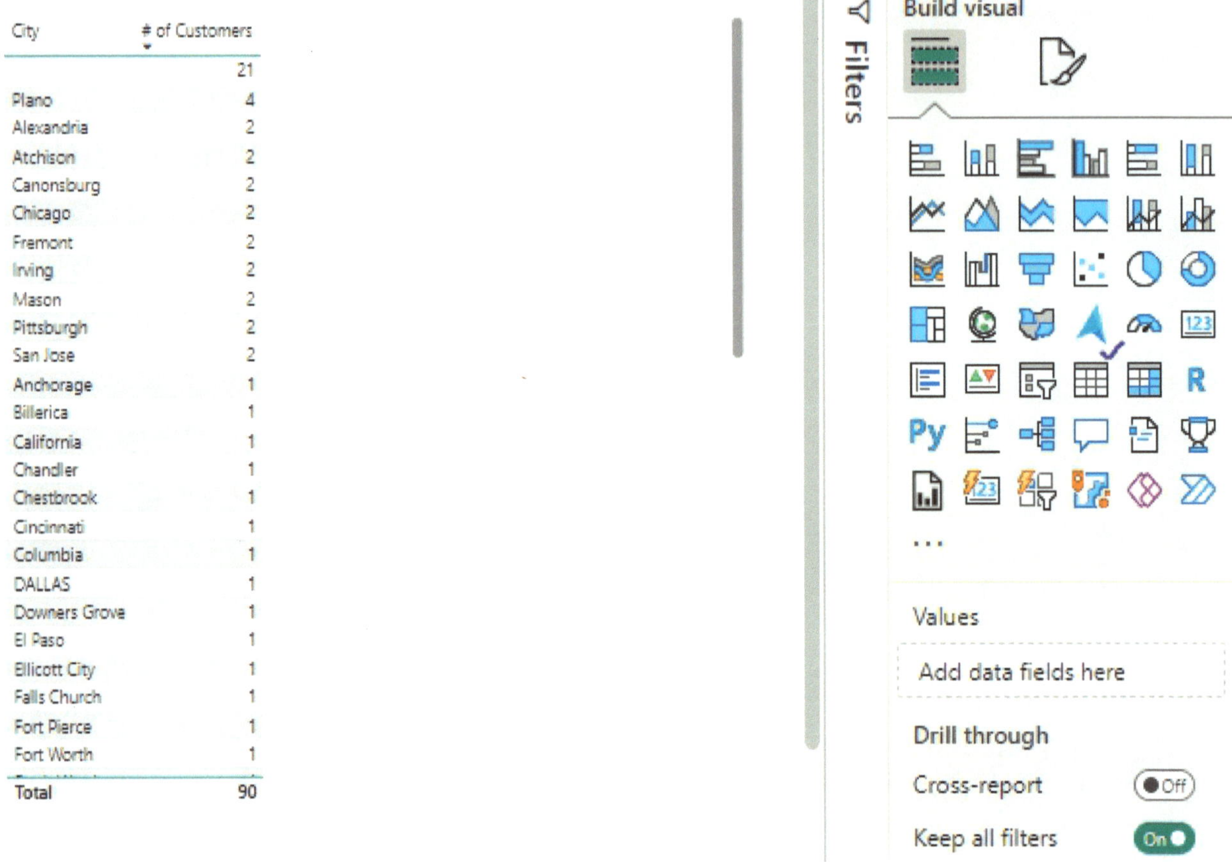

Table

6.2 Custom Visuals and Marketplace Options

Power BI's AppSource Marketplace provides access to custom visuals created by third-party developers.

Using Custom Visuals:

Navigate to the Marketplace from the Visualizations pane.

Search and import visuals like bullet charts, KPI indicators, or heatmaps.

Popular Custom Visuals:

Bullet Charts: For performance comparisons against a target.

Sunburst Charts: For hierarchical data representation.

Chiclet Slicers: For enhanced filtering options.

6.3 Formatting and Customizing Visuals

Power BI allows extensive customization to make visuals more informative and visually appealing.

6.3.1 Formatting Options

Titles and Labels: Add descriptive titles and data labels to improve clarity.

Colors and Themes: Use color schemes to align with brand guidelines or emphasize trends.

Legends: Include legends for multi-series visuals to clarify categories.

6.3.2 Interactivity

Enable cross-filtering and highlighting for better user engagement.

Configure drill-through actions to allow deeper analysis from a high-level summary.

6.3.3 Tooltips

Add tooltips to provide detailed context when hovering over a visual element.

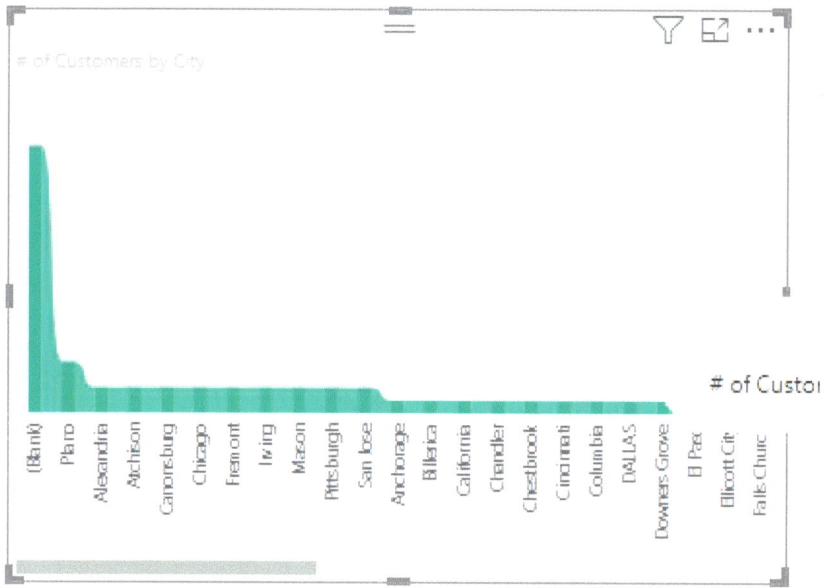

On Mouse Over Tool tip popup

6.4 Best Practices for Effective Visual Design

Designing effective visualizations requires a balance of aesthetics, clarity, and functionality.

Choose the Right Visual for the Data:

Use bar charts for comparisons, line charts for trends, and maps for geographic data.

Avoid Overloading Visuals:

Focus on one key message per visual to maintain clarity.

Emphasize Key Data:

Highlight important trends or metrics using contrasting colors or annotations.

Align Visuals Consistently:

Ensure a consistent layout, font size, and spacing across the report.

Test for Interactivity:

Verify that filters, slicers, and drill-through actions behave as expected.

Summary of Chapter 6

This chapter covered the types of visualizations available in Power BI, from basic bar charts to custom visuals. You also learned about formatting and customizing visuals to make them more engaging and informative. Finally, the chapter concluded with best practices for designing effective visuals that communicate insights clearly.

VII

Chapter 7: DAX Fundamentals

Data Analysis Expressions (DAX) is the formula language of Power BI, enabling powerful calculations and data manipulation. Mastering DAX is essential for creating insightful reports and robust data models.

7.1 Introduction to DAX (Data Analysis Expressions)

DAX is a collection of functions, operators, and constants that enable data analysis and calculations in Power BI.

Purpose: Transform raw data into actionable insights by creating calculated columns, measures, and tables.

Key Features:

Context-aware calculations.

Time intelligence for date-based analysis.

Logical operations for dynamic results.

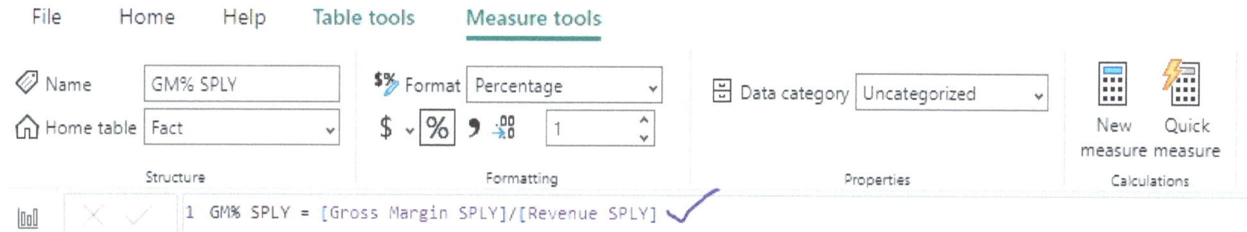

DAX formula

7.2 DAX Syntax and Operators

Understanding DAX syntax is fundamental to writing accurate and efficient formulas.

DAX Syntax:

A DAX formula begins with an equals sign = followed by the expression.

Example:

DAX

code:

"TotalSales = SUM(Sales[Amount])

   Operators in DAX:

   *Arithmetic Operators: +, -, *, /, %*

   Comparison Operators: <, >, <=, >=, =, <>

   Logical Operators: && (AND), || (OR), NOT"

7.3 Row Context vs. Filter Context

DAX operates in two primary contexts: Row Context and Filter Context.

Row Context:

Occurs when a formula evaluates a single row of data.

Example: Calculating a new column:

DAX

code:

"Profit = Sales[Amount] - Sales[Cost]"

Filter Context:

Occurs when filters are applied to tables or visuals, affecting the formula's result.

Example: A measure aggregating data based on a slicer:

DAX

Copy code

"TotalSales = SUM(Sales[Amount])"

7.4 Common DAX Functions with Examples

DAX functions can be categorized into various groups based on their purpose. Below are the most commonly used functions with examples.

7.4.1 Aggregation Functions

SUM: Calculates the total of a column.

DAX

code:

"TotalSales = SUM(Sales[Amount])"

AVERAGE: Finds the average of a column.

DAX

code:

"AvgSales = AVERAGE(Sales[Amount])"

MIN / MAX: Returns the smallest or largest value in a column.

DAX

code:

"MinSales = MIN(Sales[Amount]) MaxSales = MAX(Sales[Amount])"

7.4.2 Time Intelligence Functions

Time intelligence functions simplify date-based calculations.

DATESYTD: Calculates year-to-date totals.

DAX

code:

"YTDSales = TOTALYTD(SUM(Sales[Amount]), Sales[Date])"

SAMEPERIODLASTYEAR: Compares the same period in the previous year.

DAX

code:

“SalesLastYear = CALCULATE(SUM(Sales[Amount]), SAMEPERIODLASTYEAR(Sales[Date]))”

7.4.3 Logical and Conditional Functions

IF: Implements conditional logic.

DAX

code:

“HighSales = IF(Sales[Amount] > 10000, "High", "Low")”

SWITCH: Evaluates multiple conditions.

DAX

code:

“SalesCategory = SWITCH(TRUE(), Sales[Amount] > 10000, "High", Sales[Amount] > 5000, "Medium", "Low")”

7.4.4 Context Modification Functions

CALCULATE: Modifies the filter context for an expression.

DAX

code:

“TotalSalesEast = CALCULATE(SUM(Sales[Amount]), Sales[Region] = "East")”

FILTER: Applies a custom filter condition.

DAX

code:

“HighValueCustomers = FILTER(Customers, Customers[Revenue] > 100000)”

Summary of Chapter 7

This chapter introduced DAX fundamentals, covering its syntax, operators, and two core contexts (row and filter). It also provided detailed examples of common DAX functions, including aggregation, time intelligence, logical, and context modification functions. Understanding these concepts will empower you to create dynamic calculations and unlock deeper insights from your data.

VIII
Chapter 8: Advanced DAX

Advanced DAX techniques enable users to build more complex and efficient calculations, offering enhanced flexibility in analyzing data. This chapter covers advanced concepts like variables, iterative functions, ranking, and creating measures with multiple filters.

8.1 Using Variables in DAX
Variables improve the readability and performance of DAX formulas by storing interim results for reuse.

Syntax for Variables:
Variables are defined using the VAR keyword and must be followed by a RETURN statement.
DAX
code:

"*TotalProfitWithTax = VAR TotalSales = SUM(Sales[Amount]) VAR TotalCost = SUM(Sales[Cost]) VAR Tax = TotalSales * 0.1 RETURN TotalSales - TotalCost - Tax*"

Benefits of Using Variables:
Simplifies complex formulas by breaking them into logical steps.
Enhances performance by avoiding redundant calculations.
Improves formula readability and debugging.

8.2 Iterative Functions: SUMX, AVERAGEX
Iterative functions (also called "X" functions) operate row by row over a table, performing calculations for each row before aggregating the results.
SUMX:
The SUMX function calculates the sum of an expression evaluated for each row in a table.
DAX
code:

"*TotalRevenue = SUMX(Sales, Sales[Amount] * Sales[Quantity])*
Use Case: Calculate total revenue when individual row values require a formula."

AVERAGEX:
The AVERAGEX function calculates the average of an expression over a table.
DAX
code:

"*AvgRevenuePerUnit = AVERAGEX(Sales, Sales[Amount] / Sales[Quantity])*
Use Case: Analyze metrics that require row-level calculations, such as average sales per unit."

8.3 RANK and Ranking Techniques

Ranking techniques are essential for ordering data by metrics like sales, profit, or performance.

RANKX:

The RANKX function ranks rows based on an expression.

DAX

code:

```
"SalesRank = RANKX(ALL(Sales[Region]), SUM(Sales[Amount]), , DESC)"
```

Parameters:

ALL(Sales[Region]): Removes filters on the Region column.

SUM(Sales[Amount]): The expression to rank by.

, DESC: Specifies descending order (optional).

Dynamic Ranking:

Dynamic ranking adjusts based on slicers or filters in the report.

DAX

code:

```
"RankByProduct = RANKX(ALLSELECTED(Products), SUM(Sales[Amount]))"
```

8.4 Creating Complex Measures with Multiple Filters

Complex measures allow you to analyze data under specific conditions by combining multiple filters and context-modifying functions.

Using CALCULATE for Multiple Filters:

The CALCULATE function modifies the filter context, enabling advanced filtering scenarios.

DAX

code:

```
"HighValueSales = CALCULATE( SUM(Sales[Amount]), Sales[Amount] > 10000, Sales[Region] = "East" )"
```

Combining FILTER and CALCULATE:

To apply more dynamic conditions, use FILTER inside CALCULATE.

DAX

code:

```
"TopCustomers = CALCULATE( SUM(Sales[Amount]), FILTER(Customers, Customers[Revenue] > 50000) )"
```

Nested Measures:

Create complex measures by nesting other measures.

DAX

code:

```
"TotalProfitMargin = DIVIDE([TotalProfit], [TotalSales], 0)"
```

Summary of Chapter 8

This chapter introduced advanced DAX concepts, including the use of variables for performance and readability, iterative functions like SUMX and AVERAGEX, and ranking techniques using RANKX. It also demonstrated how to create complex measures by applying multiple filters and nesting calculations. Mastering these techniques enables analysts to handle complex scenarios and extract deeper insights from their data models.

IX

Chapter 9: Custom Columns and Measures in Power BI

Custom columns and measures in Power BI allow users to extend their datasets and create dynamic calculations. This chapter explores the differences between calculated columns and measures, provides syntax and examples, and demonstrates common business scenarios using DAX.

9.1 Understanding Calculated Columns vs. Measures

Power BI provides two main ways to add calculations to your data: calculated columns and measures.

FeatureCalculated ColumnsMeasures

ScopeOperates row-by-row in a table.Works at the aggregated level.

StorageStored in the data model, consuming space.Calculated dynamically during runtime.

Use CaseUseful for row-level transformations.Ideal for dynamic and aggregated calculations.

Example:

Calculated Column: Profit for each row.

Measure: Total profit across all rows, with slicers affecting the result.

9.2 Creating Custom Columns (Examples and Syntax)

Custom columns add new fields to a table, derived from existing data, using row-by-row logic.

Syntax for Custom Columns:

Custom columns are written in DAX and added directly in the Power BI Desktop.

9.2.1 Text Concatenation

Combine text fields or append static values.

DAX

code:

"*FullName = Customers[FirstName] & " " & Customers[LastName]*"

Use Case: Combine customer names, addresses, or any textual information.

9.2.2 Conditional Columns with IF Statements

Apply conditional logic to categorize or transform data.

DAX

code:

"*SalesCategory = IF(Sales[Amount] > 10000, "High", "Low")*"

For more complex conditions, use nested IF or SWITCH.

DAX

code:

"SalesCategory = SWITCH(TRUE(), Sales[Amount] > 10000, "High", Sales[Amount] > 5000, "Medium", "Low")"

9.3 Writing Measures with DAX

Measures are calculated at the aggregate level and are affected by slicers and filters in a report.

9.3.1 Basic Measure Examples

Total Sales:

DAX

code:

"TotalSales = SUM(Sales[Amount])"

Average Sales:

DAX

code:

"AvgSales = AVERAGE(Sales[Amount])"

Profit Margin:

DAX

code:

"ProfitMargin = DIVIDE([TotalProfit], [TotalSales], 0)"

9.3.2 Dynamic Measures Based on User Interaction

Dynamic measures adjust their values based on filters or slicers.

Sales by Selected Region:

DAX

code:

"SalesByRegion = CALCULATE(SUM(Sales[Amount]), Sales[Region] = SELECTEDVALUE(Regions[Region]))"

Top 5 Products by Sales:

DAX

code:

"Top5Products = TOPN(5, Products, [TotalSales], DESC)"

9.3.3 Example Code for Common Business Calculations

Year-over-Year Growth:

DAX

code:

"YoYGrowth = DIVIDE([TotalSales] - CALCULATE([TotalSales], SAMEPERIODLASTYEAR(Sales[Date])), CALCULATE([TotalSales], SAMEPERIODLASTYEAR(Sales[Date])), 0)"

Customer Lifetime Value:

DAX
code:

“CLV = SUMX(Customers, Customers[AverageOrderValue] * Customers[PurchaseFrequency] * Customers[CustomerLifespan])”

Revenue Per Employee:
DAX
code:

“RevenuePerEmployee = DIVIDE([TotalSales], COUNT(Employees[EmployeeID]), 0)”

Summary of Chapter 9
This chapter explored the distinction between calculated columns and measures, provided practical examples for creating custom columns using text concatenation and conditional logic, and demonstrated how to write measures for both basic and advanced calculations. By mastering these techniques, users can build robust and dynamic reports tailored to their business needs.

X

Chapter 10: Data Storytelling with Power BI Dashboards

Dashboards are the gateway to impactful data storytelling. Power BI provides powerful tools to design, customize, and share dashboards that make data-driven decisions easier. This chapter covers principles of dashboard design, adding interactivity, navigation techniques, and sharing reports effectively.

10.1 Designing a Dashboard with Purpose

A well-designed dashboard tells a story, guiding users to actionable insights.

Key Principles for Dashboard Design:

Define the Objective: Clearly understand what story your dashboard should convey.

Example: Monitor sales trends, compare regional performance, or track KPIs.

Focus on User Needs: Tailor the dashboard to your audience.

Example: Executives prefer high-level KPIs, while analysts require detailed data.

Prioritize Key Insights: Place the most important visuals at the top or center.

Choose the Right Visuals: Match data types with the best visualization.

Example: Use line charts for trends, bar charts for comparisons, and KPIs for targets.

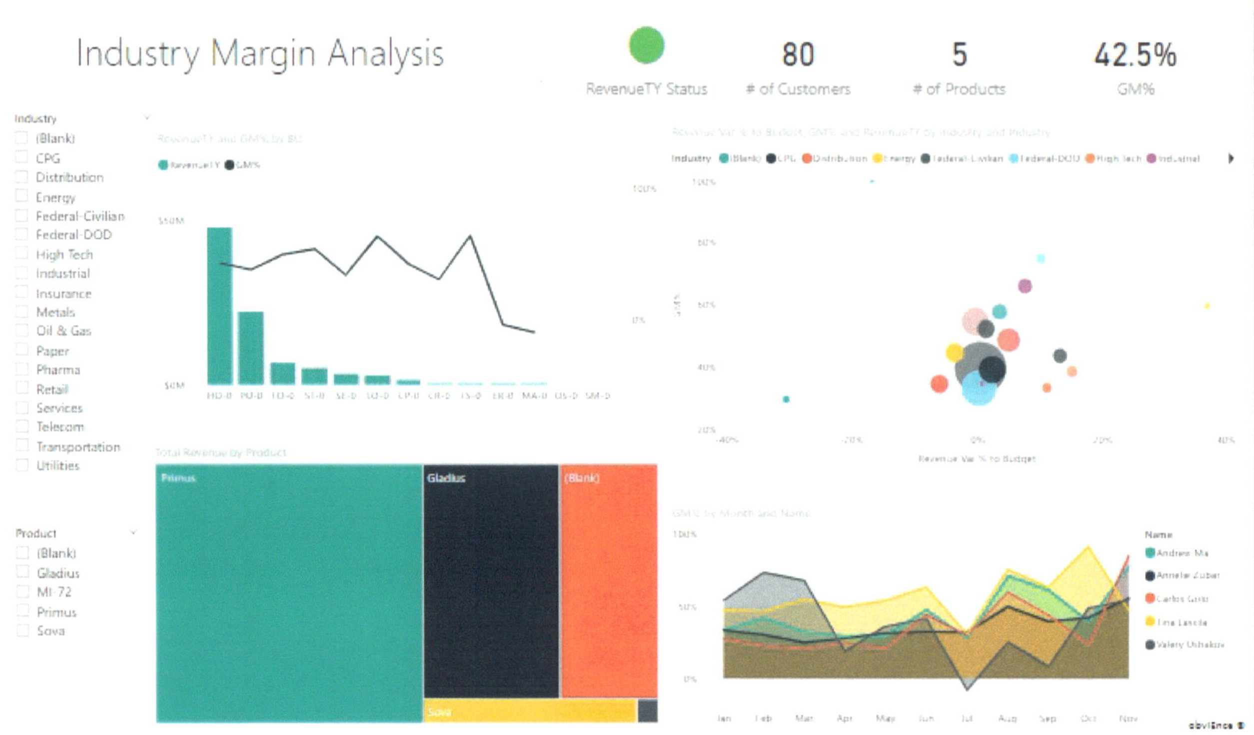

well-designed dashboard

10.2 Adding Interactivity with Slicers and Drill-throughs

Interactivity transforms dashboards from static displays into dynamic exploration tools.

Using Slicers:

Slicers allow users to filter data directly within the dashboard.

Types of Slicers:

Dropdown

List

Date Range

Example: A region slicer to filter sales data by geographical areas.

DAX

code:

```
"SelectedRegionSales = CALCULATE(SUM(Sales[Amount]), Sales[Region] = SELECTEDVALUE(Sales[Region]))"
```

Drill-throughs:

Drill-throughs enable users to navigate from summary data to detailed reports.

Setup:

Add a Drill-through page.

Drag a field to the "Drill-through" filter area.

Example: Click on a bar chart to navigate to a detailed sales report for the selected region.

10.3 Bookmarks and Report Navigation

Bookmarks save report states, enabling customized navigation experiences.

Creating Bookmarks:

Arrange visuals and slicers in the desired state.

Use the "Bookmarks" pane to save the view.

Using Buttons for Navigation:

Combine bookmarks with buttons for seamless navigation.

Example: Add a button to switch between a Sales Overview and a Profit Analysis view

10.4 Sharing and Publishing Reports

Sharing dashboards ensures collaboration and accessibility across teams.

10.4.1 Power BI Service

The Power BI Service is the primary platform for publishing, sharing, and managing reports.

Publish Reports: Upload reports from Power BI Desktop to the Power BI Service.

Create Dashboards: Pin visuals from reports to create interactive dashboards.

Share Dashboards:

Share with individual users or groups.

Set access permissions (view-only or edit)

10.4.2 Exporting and Embedding Options

Power BI offers multiple options to share reports beyond the service.

Exporting:

Export to PDF, PowerPoint, or Excel.

Use for offline sharing or presentations.

Embedding:

Embed reports in websites or applications using Power BI Embedded.

Example: Embed a sales dashboard in an internal company portal.

Public Sharing (with caution):

Publish to web for public access.

Ensure no sensitive data is exposed

Summary of Chapter 10

This chapter provided a comprehensive guide to creating engaging Power BI dashboards. From defining the purpose of your dashboard to designing interactive experiences with slicers and drill-throughs, you now have the tools to make data stories compelling and actionable. The chapter also explored navigation through bookmarks and best practices for sharing and publishing dashboards via Power BI Service and other methods.

XI

Power-BI 100 Interview Q&A

Category 1: Power BI Basics

1. **What is Power BI, and why is it used?**
   Answer:
   Power BI is a business analytics tool developed by Microsoft that provides interactive visualizations and business intelligence capabilities with an interface simple enough for end users to create their own reports and dashboards. It is used for:

   - Data analysis and visualization.
   - Building interactive dashboards.
   - Sharing insights across organizations.

2. **What are the main components of Power BI?**
   Answer:

   - **Power BI Desktop**: Used for designing reports and dashboards.
   - **Power BI Service**: A cloud-based platform to publish and share reports.
   - **Power BI Mobile**: For accessing dashboards on mobile devices.
   - **Power Query**: For data transformation.
   - **Power Pivot**: For data modeling.
   - **Power BI Report Server**: An on-premises report server.

3. **What types of data sources can Power BI connect to?**
   Answer:
   Power BI connects to over 100 data sources, including:

   - Databases: SQL Server, Oracle, MySQL, PostgreSQL.
   - Cloud services: Azure, Google Analytics, Salesforce.
   - File types: Excel, CSV, JSON, XML.
   - Live streams: IoT data, REST APIs.

Category 2: Power BI Architecture and Data Importing

1. **Explain the architecture of Power BI.**
   Answer:

Power BI architecture consists of:

- **Data Sources**: Connects to databases, files, and APIs.
- **Power Query**: Extracts, transforms, and loads (ETL) data.
- **Data Model**: Creates relationships and measures using DAX.
- **Visualization Layer**: Provides charts, KPIs, and interactive dashboards.
- **Power BI Service**: Hosts and shares reports in the cloud.

2. **What is DirectQuery, and how does it differ from Import Mode?**
   Answer:

- **Import Mode**: Data is loaded into Power BI's memory for faster performance.
- **DirectQuery**: Data remains in the source and queries are sent live, ensuring real-time updates but slower performance.

3. **What is the use of the Gateway in Power BI?**
   Answer:
   A Gateway is used to securely connect Power BI Service to on-premises data sources for data refresh or live connections.

Category 3: Data Transformation and Modeling

7. **What is Power Query, and what are its main features?**
   Answer:
   Power Query is a data connection and transformation tool. Features include:

- Data cleansing.
- Merging and appending datasets.
- Removing duplicates and nulls.
- Applying filters and custom transformations.

8. **What is a calculated column, and when should you use it?**
   Answer:
   A calculated column is created using DAX to add new fields in the data model. It is used for row-by-row calculations, such as:

```DAX
Copy code
FullName = Customers[FirstName] & " " & Customers[LastName]
```

9. **Explain the difference between star schema and snowflake schema in Power BI.**
   Answer:

- **Star Schema**: Simplified with fact tables at the center and directly related dimension tables.
- **Snowflake Schema**: More normalized with dimensions split into sub-dimensions.

Category 4: DAX (Data Analysis Expressions)

10. **What is DAX, and why is it important?**
    Answer:
    DAX is a formula language in Power BI used for creating custom calculations. It is essential for:

    - Creating measures and calculated columns.
    - Manipulating data in the model.
    - Performing advanced analytics, such as time intelligence.

11. **What is the difference between SUM and SUMX in DAX?**
    Answer:

    - **SUM**: Adds all values in a column.
    - **SUMX**: Iterates row by row, performing calculations for each row.

12. **What are row context and filter context in DAX?**
    Answer:

    - **Row Context**: Applies to calculated columns and iterates row by row.
    - **Filter Context**: Applies to measures and considers slicers, filters, or report contexts.

Category 5: Visualizations

13. **What are the different types of visuals available in Power BI?**
    Answer:

    - Standard: Bar charts, line charts, pie charts, maps, scatter plots, tables.
    - Custom visuals: Downloadable from the Power BI marketplace.

14. **How can you create a hierarchy in Power BI?**
    Answer:
    Drag fields (e.g., Year, Month, Day) into the same column in the "Fields" pane to automatically create a hierarchy for drill-down.

15. **What are tooltips in Power BI?**
    Answer:
    Tooltips display additional information when hovering over a visual. You can customize tooltips with fields and measures.

Category 6: Power BI Service and Sharing

16. **What is the difference between a report and a dashboard in Power BI?**
    Answer:

    - **Report**: A multi-page collection of visuals, created in Power BI Desktop.
    - **Dashboard**: A single-page summary with pinned visuals, created in Power BI Service.

17. **How do you share Power BI dashboards?**
    Answer:
    Share dashboards via Power BI Service by:

- Using the "Share" button.
- Embedding in applications or websites.
- Exporting to PDF/PowerPoint.

Category 7: Advanced DAX and Calculations

18. **What is the difference between a calculated column and a measure?**
    Answer:

- **Calculated Column**: Calculated row by row during data load and stored in the model.
- **Measure**: Calculated dynamically based on the filter context during report execution.

19. **How do you perform Time Intelligence in DAX?**
    Answer:
    Time Intelligence functions allow comparisons across different time periods. Examples include:

- **DATESYTD**: Calculates year-to-date values.
- **SAMEPERIODLASTYEAR**: Compares the same period from the previous year.
    Example:

```DAX
Copy code
SalesYTD = TOTALYTD(SUM(Sales[Amount]), Dates[Date])
```

20. **What is the purpose of the CALCULATE function in DAX?**
    Answer:
    CALCULATE evaluates an expression in a modified filter context. It changes the context of a calculation.
    Example:

```DAX
Copy code
SalesUS = CALCULATE(SUM(Sales[Amount]), Sales[Region] = "US")
```

21. **What is the use of the FILTER function in DAX?**
    Answer:
    FILTER allows you to return a table based on a condition, often used with CALCULATE to modify the context.
    Example:

```DAX
Copy code
SalesGreaterThan1000 = CALCULATE(SUM(Sales[Amount]), FILTER(Sales, Sales[Amount] > 1000))
```

22. **What are iterators in DAX?**
    Answer:
    Iterators are functions that perform calculations row by row, such as **SUMX**, **AVERAGEX**, and **COUNTX**. They iterate over a table and return the result.
    Example:

DAX
Copy code
TotalRevenue = SUMX(Sales, Sales[Quantity] * Sales[Price])

23. **How do you calculate a running total in DAX?**
Answer:
A running total can be calculated using the **CALCULATE** function in conjunction with **FILTER** to accumulate the values over time.
Example:

DAX
Copy code
RunningTotal = CALCULATE(SUM(Sales[Amount]), FILTER(ALL(Dates), Dates[Date] <= MAX(Dates[Date])))

24. **What is the difference between DISTINCT and VALUES in DAX?**
Answer:

- **DISTINCT**: Returns a table with unique values from a column.
- **VALUES**: Returns a table with distinct values but can also handle blanks.
  Example:

DAX
Copy code
UniqueProducts = DISTINCT(Sales[Product])
Category 8: Power BI Service, Sharing, and Collaboration

25. **What are workspaces in Power BI?**
Answer:
Workspaces are containers in the Power BI Service where teams can collaborate on datasets, reports, and dashboards. They allow users to share content securely within a group.

26. **What is a Power BI App?**
Answer:
A Power BI App is a collection of dashboards, reports, and datasets bundled together for easy access and distribution. They can be published and shared with users or groups.

27. **What is Row-Level Security (RLS) in Power BI?**
Answer:
Row-Level Security (RLS) restricts data access for certain users by creating security roles and applying filters to restrict the data they can see in reports.
Example:

DAX
Copy code
[Region] = USERNAME()

28. **How do you set up RLS in Power BI?**
Answer:
RLS is set up in Power BI Desktop by creating security roles and using DAX expressions to filter data. Once the roles are defined, they can be published to Power BI Service.

29. **What is a Power BI Gateway, and when is it used?**
    Answer:
    A Power BI Gateway is used to provide secure data transfer between on-premises data sources and the Power BI Service. It allows for data refreshes and live queries in cloud-based reports.
30. **How do you refresh a dataset in Power BI?**
    Answer:
    Datasets in Power BI can be refreshed automatically or manually via the Power BI Service. Scheduled refresh allows you to keep data up-to-date without manual intervention.
31. **What is the difference between a Power BI Pro and Power BI Premium?**
    Answer:

   - **Power BI Pro**: Designed for individuals and teams with sharing, collaboration, and content publishing capabilities.
   - **Power BI Premium**: Offers dedicated cloud resources, larger storage capacity, and more advanced features like paginated reports and AI integration.

Category 9: Power BI Performance Optimization

32. **How can you improve the performance of a Power BI report?**
    Answer:

   - Reduce the amount of data by filtering unnecessary rows.
   - Use aggregation tables for large datasets.
   - Optimize DAX calculations and use variables to store intermediate results.
   - Minimize the use of complex visuals or reduce the number of visuals on a page.

33. **What is query folding in Power BI?**
    Answer:
    Query folding is when Power Query sends data transformation logic to the source system rather than loading all data into memory, thus improving performance.
34. **How can you handle large datasets in Power BI?**
    Answer:

   - Use DirectQuery mode for real-time data access.
   - Implement aggregation tables for summarizing data before loading it into the model.
   - Use incremental data refresh to load only the new or updated data.

35. **What is the importance of relationships in Power BI?**
    Answer:
    Relationships define how tables are connected in Power BI, enabling you to model and analyze data across different sources. Proper relationships are critical for accurate reporting and calculations.

Category 10: Power BI Advanced Features

36. **What is Power BI Embedded?**
    Answer:
    Power BI Embedded allows developers to embed interactive Power BI reports and dashboards into custom applications for end-users without requiring a Power BI account.

37. **What are custom visuals in Power BI?**
    Answer:
    Custom visuals are third-party visuals available in the Power BI marketplace that can be used to extend Power BI's native visual options. They are created using JavaScript and can be customized for specific use cases.

38. **What is Power Automate, and how does it integrate with Power BI?**
    Answer:
    Power Automate is a cloud-based service that allows users to automate workflows between apps and services. It can be integrated with Power BI to trigger alerts, refresh datasets, or send notifications based on data changes.

39. **How can you use Power BI with Excel?**
    Answer:

- **Export Data**: Export data from Power BI to Excel for detailed analysis.
- **Power BI Publisher for Excel**: Pin Excel ranges as tiles in Power BI dashboards.
- **Power BI for Excel Add-in**: Analyze Power BI data directly within Excel using the add-in.

40. **What is a paginated report in Power BI?**
    Answer:
    Paginated reports are highly formatted reports designed for printing or exporting. Unlike interactive reports, these reports can span multiple pages and are optimized for specific formatting needs.

Category 11: Power BI Advanced Features (Continued)

41. **What is the difference between Power BI Pro and Power BI Premium Per User (PPU)?**
    Answer:

- **Power BI Pro**: Licenses for individuals to create, share, and collaborate on content.
- **Power BI Premium Per User (PPU)**: Provides premium capabilities for individual users with additional features such as large model sizes, AI integration, and paginated reports.

42. **How can you schedule a data refresh in Power BI Service?**
    Answer:
    You can schedule data refresh by:

- Going to **Power BI Service** > **Settings** > **Datasets**.
- Under **Scheduled refresh**, enable it and configure the refresh frequency (daily, weekly, etc.).

43. **What is the "Power BI Gateway"? What is its role in data refresh?**
    Answer:
    The **Power BI Gateway** acts as a bridge between Power BI Service and on-premises data sources for real-time data access and automatic refreshes. There are two types:

- **Personal Gateway**: For personal use, supporting data refreshes only from a single PC.
- **Enterprise Gateway**: For organizational use, supporting multiple data sources and scheduled refreshes.

44. **What is a "composite model" in Power BI?**
    Answer:
    A composite model allows you to combine data from different storage modes (e.g., DirectQuery and Import) in a single report. This enables greater flexibility in managing real-time and static data.

45. **What are "Dynamic Security" and "Row-Level Security" in Power BI?**
Answer:

- **Row-Level Security (RLS)**: Restricts access to data at the row level based on the user's identity or role.
- **Dynamic Security**: A more flexible form of RLS that can use dynamic filters, based on a table or external data, to apply security settings dynamically.

46. **How can you handle missing or NULL values in Power BI?**
Answer:

- Replace NULL values using **Power Query** with the **Replace Values** option.
- Use **DAX** functions such as **IFERROR, COALESCE,** or **ISBLANK** to handle NULL values in measures or calculated columns.
  Example:

```DAX
Copy code
CleanedSales = IF(ISBLANK(Sales[Amount]), 0, Sales[Amount])
```

47. **Explain Power BI's support for integration with AI capabilities.**
Answer:
Power BI integrates with Azure AI to add features such as:

- **AI visuals** like key influencers, decomposition trees, and smart narratives.
- **Cognitive services** to apply text analytics or image recognition.
- **Azure Machine Learning** integration for predictive modeling.

Category 12: Power BI Best Practices and Report Design

48. **What are some best practices for designing Power BI reports?**
Answer:

- Keep the report simple and intuitive for the user.
- Use filters and slicers effectively for interactivity.
- Optimize visuals to avoid overloading the report page.
- Consistently use colors, fonts, and layouts to maintain visual harmony.
- Use tooltips for additional information.
- Apply good data modeling techniques to improve performance.

49. **What is the importance of defining KPIs in Power BI?**
Answer:
KPIs (Key Performance Indicators) are essential for tracking business performance. They help stakeholders quickly assess whether the business is meeting its goals. Power BI allows you to define KPIs by combining values, targets, and thresholds in your visualizations.

50. **How do you create a dashboard in Power BI Service?**
Answer:

- Pin visualizations from reports to the dashboard by clicking **Pin** on individual visuals.

- Customize the layout and arrange visuals on a single page.
- Dashboards can also be shared with other users or groups once created.

51. **What are bookmarks in Power BI, and how are they used?**
Answer:
Bookmarks capture the current state of a report page, including filters, slicers, and visuals. They are used for creating storytelling elements or interactive navigation. You can use bookmarks for:

- Report navigation.
- Creating guided reports.
- Retaining user selections across pages.

52. **What are slicers in Power BI, and how do they work?**
Answer:
Slicers are visual filters that allow users to select and filter data interactively. Slicers can be used to filter data by categories, such as time periods, regions, or product groups. They enhance user experience and interactivity.

53. **How do you improve the user experience when designing Power BI reports?**
Answer:

- Keep the layout clean and intuitive.
- Provide contextual filters and slicers for easy navigation.
- Minimize the number of visuals on a page to reduce clutter.
- Ensure that the report is mobile-friendly.
- Use the "Focus Mode" to allow detailed analysis of visuals.

54. **What is the difference between a clustered bar chart and a stacked bar chart in Power BI?**
Answer:

- **Clustered Bar Chart**: Displays individual bars side by side for comparison.
- **Stacked Bar Chart**: Combines different values within a single bar, stacked on top of one another, to show the total and individual contributions.

Category 13: Power BI Integration and Data Management

55. **What is Power BI's integration with Excel?**
Answer:

- **Exporting**: Power BI allows exporting data and visuals to Excel.
- **Power Query**: Users can access Power BI queries and data in Excel via the Power BI Publisher for Excel.
- **Analyze in Excel**: A feature that allows users to create Excel-based reports using Power BI data models.

56. **How do you integrate Power BI with SharePoint?**
Answer:
Power BI can be integrated with SharePoint by embedding reports directly in SharePoint Online. You can use the **Power BI Web Part** to display reports and dashboards in SharePoint pages.

57. **What is Power BI's integration with Microsoft Teams?**
Answer:

- Power BI can be integrated directly into Microsoft Teams by adding Power BI tabs in channels.
- This integration allows users to share reports, collaborate on insights, and track progress without leaving Teams.

58. **How can you handle incremental data refresh in Power BI?**
Answer:
Incremental data refresh allows for refreshing only new or updated data rather than the entire dataset. This improves performance and reduces refresh time, particularly for large datasets. It's configured in the **Power BI Service**.

59. **What is Power BI Dataflow, and how is it different from Power Query?**
Answer:
Power BI Dataflows are a cloud-based ETL (Extract, Transform, Load) service in Power BI. They allow you to transform, clean, and store data in the cloud. Dataflows can be reused across reports and datasets, unlike Power Query, which is primarily used in Power BI Desktop for individual reports.

60. **What is Power BI's integration with SQL Server Analysis Services (SSAS)?**
Answer:
Power BI integrates with SSAS for reporting and analysis of OLAP cubes and tabular models. You can connect Power BI directly to SSAS using **Live Connections** to retrieve data and build reports.

Category 14: Power BI Governance and Security

61. **What are the different types of Power BI permissions?**
Answer:

- **Admin**: Full control over the workspace, including content management and security settings.
- **Member**: Can edit and share content within the workspace.
- **Contributor**: Can create and modify reports but cannot delete or manage workspace content.
- **Viewer**: Can only view the content within the workspace.

62. **What is Data Loss Prevention (DLP) in Power BI?**
Answer:
DLP policies in Power BI allow organizations to set up rules to prevent sensitive data from being shared inappropriately. These policies can be enforced through the Power BI Admin portal.

63. **How do you manage Power BI security using Azure Active Directory (AAD)?**
Answer:
Power BI integrates with **Azure Active Directory (AAD)** for user authentication and access control. AAD groups can be used to manage user access to workspaces, reports, and dashboards in Power BI.

64. **What is a service principal in Power BI?**
Answer:
A **Service Principal** is an identity used by applications or services to interact with Power BI resources without requiring a specific user login. It's often used in automation scenarios such as data refreshes or embedded analytics.

65. **How can you audit Power BI activities?**
Answer:
You can use the **Power BI Audit Logs** to track user activities such as viewing, sharing, and exporting reports, or downloading datasets. These logs are available via the **Power BI Admin Portal** and can be exported to external systems for analysis.

Category 15: Power BI Advanced Data Visualization Techniques

66. **What is the use of custom visuals in Power BI?**
Answer:
Custom visuals are third-party visuals that extend Power BI's default visualization options. They are available in the Power BI Marketplace and can provide specialized functionality or enhanced design features.

67. **How do you create a waterfall chart in Power BI?**
Answer:
The waterfall chart shows cumulative data and helps in understanding the incremental effect of sequential values. It can be created by selecting **Waterfall Chart** from the visualization pane and configuring the axis and value fields.

68. **What is a decomposed tree in Power BI?**
Answer:
The decomposed tree visual is used to break down a measure into its components. It helps to see how each factor contributes to the overall value. For example, decomposing sales to see contributions from different regions and products.

69. **Explain how Power BI integrates with map visuals.**
Answer:
Power BI supports map visualizations for spatial data analysis. You can use **basic maps**, **filled maps**, or **ArcGIS maps** to plot geographic data. Power BI uses latitude and longitude coordinates for mapping data to geographic locations.

Category 16: Power BI Performance Optimization

70. **How can you optimize Power BI reports for performance?**
Answer:

- **Data Reduction**: Filter unnecessary data during import.
- **Aggregations**: Use aggregate tables to reduce the data granularity.
- **Minimize the use of calculated columns**: Use measures instead as they perform better.
- **Avoid complex DAX**: Keep DAX expressions simple to improve performance.
- **Disable auto date/time**: Turn off auto date/time for better performance.
- **Optimize visuals**: Use fewer visuals and avoid highly complex visualizations.

71. **What is the impact of using DirectQuery on Power BI performance?**
Answer:
DirectQuery allows Power BI to query data directly from the data source, but it can slow down performance since each interaction with the report results in a query to the data source. It's crucial to ensure the source system can handle the additional load, and appropriate indexes should be used.

72. **How can you reduce the size of Power BI data models?**
Answer:

- **Remove unnecessary columns and tables** from the model.
- **Use star schema** or other efficient modeling techniques.
- **Compress data** by converting it into more efficient formats like integers or dates.
- **Limit cardinality** of columns in the model.
- **Use incremental refresh** for large datasets.

73. **What are the best practices for creating efficient DAX measures?**
Answer:

- Use **SUMX**, **AVERAGEX** and similar iterator functions only when necessary.
- Avoid using **CALCULATE** too frequently as it can cause performance issues.
- Use **variables** to store intermediate results in complex calculations.
- Use the **ALL** function wisely to remove unwanted filters without overcomplicating the DAX expression.
- Optimize the granularity of your model to avoid using high-cardinality columns in measures.

74. **What is a Power BI Aggregation Table? How can it improve performance?**
Answer:

Aggregation tables are pre-calculated summaries of data at a higher level of granularity. When queried, Power BI can use these aggregated tables to return results faster rather than querying the entire dataset. This can significantly improve performance for large datasets.

Category 17: Power BI and Cloud Services

75. **What is Power BI Embedded, and how does it work?**
Answer:

Power BI Embedded is a service that allows developers to embed Power BI reports, dashboards, and visuals into external applications, websites, or portals. It is typically used by independent software vendors (ISVs) or developers who need to deliver embedded analytics to their customers.

76. **How does Power BI integrate with Azure?**
Answer:

Power BI integrates with Azure in various ways:

- **Azure Data Services**: Power BI can connect directly to Azure data services like Azure SQL Database, Azure Synapse Analytics, and more.
- **Azure Machine Learning**: Integration allows you to apply machine learning models to your Power BI data.
- **Azure Data Lake**: Data can be stored and analyzed using Power BI from the Azure Data Lake.

77. **What is Power BI's connection with Azure Synapse Analytics?**
Answer:

Power BI integrates with **Azure Synapse Analytics** to provide seamless data exploration and reporting from large-scale data warehouse systems. Power BI can pull data from Synapse directly, allowing for real-time analytics and reporting on big data.

78. **What are the Power BI integration capabilities with Microsoft Dynamics 365?**
Answer:

Power BI integrates with **Microsoft Dynamics 365** to visualize and analyze business data. This integration provides pre-built dashboards and reports for sales, finance, and operations, as well as the ability to create custom reports and queries.

79. **How does Power BI integrate with Google Analytics?**
Answer:

Power BI connects to **Google Analytics** via a built-in connector, enabling users to import data about website traffic, user behavior, and conversions. This data can then be analyzed and visualized in Power BI reports and dashboards.

Category 18: Power BI Advanced Visualization and Customization

80. **How do you create a custom visual in Power BI?**
Answer:

- Use the **Power BI Custom Visuals SDK** to create a custom visual.
- Create your visual in **JavaScript** and **TypeScript**.
- Deploy the visual to the **AppSource** marketplace or import it into your report.
- Custom visuals can be downloaded from the Power BI Marketplace or created from scratch using the SDK.

81. **How do you apply conditional formatting to a Power BI table or matrix?**
    Answer:
    Conditional formatting can be applied by right-clicking on a field in the table or matrix and selecting **Conditional formatting**. You can choose to format based on field values, such as changing cell color, font size, or applying data bars.

82. **What is a KPI (Key Performance Indicator) visual in Power BI?**
    Answer:
    A KPI visual in Power BI is used to display key performance indicators in a compact and visually intuitive format. It shows the progress of a metric against a target value, with a color-coded indicator to denote whether the KPI has been met.

83. **What is a "decomposition tree" visual in Power BI?**
    Answer:
    The **decomposition tree** visual allows you to break down a measure into its contributing factors. It helps to identify the root causes or drivers behind a value, such as revenue, by drilling down into categories like region, product, or customer.

84. **How can you use a waterfall chart in Power BI?****
    Answer:
    The **waterfall chart** shows sequential data points that help in visualizing cumulative effects. It's used to display how an initial value is affected by a series of positive or negative values, such as tracking sales over time by regions or product categories.

85. **What is a sankey diagram and how is it used in Power BI?**
    Answer:
    A **sankey diagram** is a flow diagram that visualizes the flow of data between different categories. It is typically used to show proportional relationships or the transfer of data from one category to another, like revenue flows across departments or customer movement through a funnel.

Category 19: Power BI Security and Access Management

86. **What is Row-Level Security (RLS) and how is it implemented?**
    Answer:
    Row-Level Security (RLS) restricts data access for users based on roles or filters. It can be implemented in Power BI by:

- Defining security roles in **Power BI Desktop**.
- Using DAX to filter data based on user identities (via **USERNAME()** function).
- Assigning roles to users in Power BI Service.

87. **How do you grant access to a Power BI report or dashboard?**
    Answer:
    You can grant access to a Power BI report or dashboard by:

- **Sharing**: Send the report link directly to users or groups.
- **Publish to Web**: Share the report publicly via a URL (not recommended for sensitive data).

- **Power BI Service**: Add users to workspaces and grant permissions (Viewer, Contributor, Admin).

88. **What is the Power BI Service Principal and how does it work in security?**
   Answer:
   A **Service Principal** is used to automate access to Power BI resources via APIs or services. It is an identity used by services or applications to connect to Power BI without needing a user's credentials.

89. **How do you manage Power BI permissions within a workspace?**
   Answer:

   - **Admins** can manage the workspace, add members, and control access.
   - **Members** can edit reports and datasets.
   - **Contributors** can modify reports but not manage workspace settings.
   - **Viewers** can only view reports and dashboards within the workspace.

90. **What are the different sharing options in Power BI?**
   Answer:
   Power BI offers several sharing options:

   - **Direct Sharing**: Send a report or dashboard link to individual users or groups.
   - **Publish to Web**: Make the report public by generating a shareable URL.
   - **Power BI Apps**: Create a packaged report for organizational distribution.
   - **Embedding**: Embed Power BI content into websites or applications.

   Category 20: Power BI Integration with Other Technologies

91. **How do you connect Power BI to SQL Server?**
   Answer:
   You can connect Power BI to SQL Server by selecting **Get Data** > **SQL Server** and providing the server and database name. You can choose between **Import** or **DirectQuery** depending on your requirements.

92. **How do you perform data transformation in Power BI?**
   Answer:
   Data transformation in Power BI is done using **Power Query Editor**. You can perform transformations such as filtering rows, changing column types, merging tables, and applying custom calculations using the **M language**.

93. **What is the difference between Power BI and Power Pivot?**
   Answer:
   Power Pivot is an Excel add-in for creating data models, whereas Power BI is a standalone BI tool that provides end-to-end analytics and visualizations. Power BI includes the features of Power Pivot but extends them to support collaboration, sharing, and online publishing.

94. **Can Power BI connect to Google BigQuery?**
   Answer:
   Yes, Power BI can connect to **Google BigQuery** using the BigQuery connector. You need to authenticate and grant access, then you can pull data from your BigQuery tables into Power BI for analysis.

   Category 21: Power BI Certification and Learning

95. **What are the prerequisites for Power BI Certification?**
   Answer:
   The **Power BI Certification** (DA-100: Analyzing Data with Power BI) does not have specific prerequisites. However,

experience with Power BI Desktop, DAX, Power Query, and report creation is highly recommended.

96. **How can you get started with learning Power BI?**
Answer:
Start with Microsoft's official **Power BI Learning Path** and explore the many online courses, tutorials, and community resources available. Practice by working with real datasets and building reports.

97. **How do you troubleshoot common issues in Power BI?**
Answer:
Troubleshooting Power BI can include:

- Checking **error messages** in the Power Query editor.
- Using **Performance Analyzer** to diagnose performance issues.
- Ensuring data model relationships are correctly configured.
- Verifying **data refresh** and permissions issues.

98. **What is the Power BI Community, and why is it important?**
Answer:
The **Power BI Community** is a place where users can ask questions, share insights, and collaborate. It is valuable for learning new techniques, troubleshooting, and staying updated with Power BI's latest features and releases.

99. **How do you stay updated with new Power BI features?**
Answer:
Stay updated by subscribing to the **Power BI Blog**, attending **Power BI Webinars**, and joining the **Power BI Community**. Microsoft also announces major updates via the **Power BI Release Notes**.

100. **What are the career opportunities for Power BI professionals?**
Answer:
Careers for Power BI professionals include roles such as **Data Analyst**, **Business Intelligence Analyst**, **Power BI Developer**, **Data Scientist**, and **BI Consultant**. Power BI expertise is in high demand in industries ranging from finance to healthcare, retail, and technology.

This book has provided a detailed journey through Power BI, equipping readers with the knowledge to master data analysis and visualization. Below is a summary of the key insights from each chapter:

Power BI Architecture and Data Importing Techniques:

Explored Power BI's architecture and introduced various methods to import data from multiple sources effectively.

Data Transformation Techniques:

Focused on cleaning, shaping, and preparing data with Power Query, emphasizing efficiency in handling raw datasets.

Data Modeling Fundamentals:

Discussed creating relationships between tables, managing cardinality, and best practices for a robust data model.

Optimizing Table Relationships and Advanced Modeling:

Delved into advanced modeling techniques like bi-directional filtering, role-playing dimensions, and hierarchical structures.

Power BI Interface and Components:

Provided a detailed walkthrough of the Power BI Desktop, Service, and Mobile interfaces.

Visualizations in Power BI:

Covered a wide array of built-in and custom visuals, along with formatting and design best practices.

DAX Fundamentals:

Introduced the basics of Data Analysis Expressions (DAX), its syntax, and commonly used functions.

Advanced DAX:

Expanded on DAX with topics like variables, iterative functions, ranking, and complex calculations.

Custom Columns and Measures:

Explained how to create calculated columns and measures, along with practical business use cases.

Data Storytelling with Power BI Dashboards:

Highlighted dashboard design, interactivity through slicers and drill-throughs, bookmarks, and sharing strategies.

By mastering the concepts in these chapters, readers are equipped to design scalable data solutions, build impactful reports, and tell compelling stories with their data.

The Analytical Future in IT

The IT industry is rapidly evolving, and analytics is at the forefront of this transformation. Here are the key trends shaping the future of analytics:

1. Artificial Intelligence and Machine Learning Integration

AI and ML are no longer standalone technologies—they are becoming integral to analytics platforms. Tools like Power BI are incorporating AI capabilities, such as:

Automated insights generation.

Natural language processing (e.g., Q&A in Power BI).

Predictive analytics for forecasting trends.

2. Real-Time Analytics

With the rise of IoT and big data, organizations are moving toward real-time data processing. Analytics platforms will increasingly offer live dashboards, instant alerts, and streaming data insights.

3. Augmented Analytics

Augmented analytics, driven by AI, will empower users by automating data preparation, insight generation, and storytelling. This shift reduces dependency on specialized data analysts.

4. Cloud-Native Solutions

The migration to cloud-based platforms like Power BI Service is accelerating. The cloud offers scalability, accessibility, and integration with other cloud services, making analytics more collaborative and dynamic.

5. Embedded Analytics

Businesses are embedding analytics into their applications to make insights more accessible and actionable at the point of decision-making. Power BI Embedded is an example of this trend.

6. Democratization of Data

Organizations are investing in self-service analytics tools like Power BI to empower non-technical users. This democratization fosters a data-driven culture across all levels of the enterprise.

7. Data Governance and Security

As analytics becomes more pervasive, ensuring data accuracy, compliance, and security is critical. Future analytics platforms will integrate advanced governance frameworks.

CONCLUSION

Becoming a Data Analyst:

The IT industry is heading toward a future where data analysts every decision. As a Power BI expert, you are now equipped with the skills to:

- Transform raw data into actionable insights.
- Build scalable and secure data models.
- Create compelling stories that drive business outcomes.

By staying updated with trends like AI integration, real-time analytics, and cloud-based solutions, you can remain a leader in the evolving analytics landscape. The knowledge gained from this book is your foundation to succeed in the data-driven world of tomorrow.

All The Best ....Happy Learning!!

www.ingramcontent.com/pod-product-compliance
Lightning Source LLC
Chambersburg PA
CBHW041642110726
48005CB00003B/681